Alfred's

Teach Yourself To Play Banjo

● ●

MORTY MANUS
RON MANUS

Everything you need to know to start playing the 5-string banjo now!

In addition to video lessons, the companion DVD includes Alfred's exclusive TNT 2 software which allows users to customize the audio tracks in this book for practice. Use it to slow down tracks, isolate and loop parts, and change tempos and keys.

To install, insert the DVD into the disc drive of your computer.

Windows
Double-click on **My Computer**, right-click on the DVD drive icon, and select **Explore**. Open the **DVD-ROM Materials** folder, then the **TnT2** folder, then the **Windows** folder, and double-click on the installer file.

Macintosh
Double-click on the DVD icon on your desktop. Open the **DVD-ROM Materials** folder, then the **TnT2** folder, then the **Mac** folder, and double-click on the installer file.

TNT 2 SYSTEM REQUIREMENTS

Windows	**Macintosh**
XP, Vista, 7, 8	OS 10.4 and higher (Intel only)
QuickTime 7.6.7 or higher	QuickTime 7.6.7 or higher
1.8 GHz processor or faster	1.1 GB hard drive space
1.1 GB hard drive space	2 GB RAM minimum
2 GB RAM minimum	DVD drive for installation
DVD drive for installation	Speakers or headphones
Speakers or headphones	Internet access for updates
Internet access for updates	

Alfred Music
P.O. Box 10003
Van Nuys, CA 91410-0003
alfred.com

Copyright © MMXIV by Alfred Music
All rights reserved. Printed in USA.

ISBN-10: 1-4706-1531-2 (Book & CD & DVD)
ISBN-13: 978-1-4706-1531-4 (Book & CD & DVD)

Audio recording performed by Scott Linford.

Cover photo courtesy of Gibson USA

 Alfred Cares. Contents printed on environmentally responsible paper.

CONTENTS

GETTING STARTED

A SHORT HISTORY OF THE BANJO

There are four types of banjos in common use: the four-string, short-neck tenor; the four-string long-neck plectrum; the six-string banjo tuned like a guitar; and the one this book will teach you how to play, the five-string banjo.

Banjos were brought to America by West Africans who played an instrument called the *bania*. They may have adapted the bania from similar stringed instruments they heard the Arabs playing. The bania has several strings stretched over a wooden neck and hollow gourd, which acted as a resonator. Early in the development of the instrument its resonance was improved by slicing a piece off the side of the gourd and stretching an animal skin over the resulting hole. It is this skin (now usually made of plastic) that gives the banjo its characteristic bright, "snappy" sound.

The earliest American banjos that still exist date from about 1830. Soon after that an important improvement and a brilliant innovation permitted players to reach the heights of technique previously unheard of: the improvement was the addition of frets (which early banjo makers borrowed from the guitar and mandolin) and the innovation was the addition of a fifth string. Unlike the four longer strings, however, the fifth string is a short *drone* string, which means that no matter what else is being played, the fifth string always sounds the same note, either the root or the fifth of the key. One possibility is that this innovation was an attempt by American banjo players of Scottish-Irish ancestry to imitate the sound of the bagpipe*

*Bagpipes have one or more drone pipes that sound the same note regardless of what else is being played. The melody is played on different pipes, called *chanters*. The modern banjo player gets a comparable effect by playing the melody on the four long strings while the short fifth string continually sounds the same note.

which was such an important part of their musical culture. There is also evidence the fifth string dates back to the instrument's African roots.

Surprisingly, the five-string banjo was often used in the 19th century for playing classical melodies. There is much printed music from the period 1875 to about 1910 that proves that the instrument was in great demand for this purpose. (To hear what this sounded like, listen to the historic recordings of banjo virtuoso Fred van Epps, who recorded before the first World War.)

Although it had always been popular as a folk instrument, the banjo really came into its own with the beginnings of bluegrass music in the late 1920s. The basic bluegrass band consists of five instruments: fiddle, mandolin, bass, guitar and five-string banjo. (It is said that the early bluegrass musicians were using stringed instruments to imitate the sounds of Dixieland jazz they heard on radio.)

Bluegrass soon became an independent, important and exciting part of the American music scene. Banjo pickers like Earl Scruggs, Don Reno, Bobby Thompson and many others brought the instrument to new heights of virtuosity, and innovators like Dick Weissman and the incredible Bela Fleck continue to push the boundaries of what the instrument can do.

In this book we will give you a thorough grounding in the basics of five-string banjo playing. No matter whether your interest lies in bluegrass, folk, jazz or even classical, the fundamentals of playing the instrument are the same. After completing *Teach Yourself to Play 5-String Banjo*, you'll be on your way to becoming an excellent player in your favorite musical style!

Earl Scruggs, here with his partner Lester Flatt and their band, is famous for his three-finger style of playing. He also invented the "Scruggs peg," a device used for making quick changes in tuning of B and G strings. *Photo courtesy of Country Music Foundation.*

THE 5-STRING BANJO

Important note: As mentioned on page 3, there are many different types of banjos. This book is meant only for the 5-String banjo! Make sure you have a banjo that has four long strings, plus a short fifth string that ends at about the fifth fret. If you have a 4- or 6-String banjo, you won't be able to use this book.

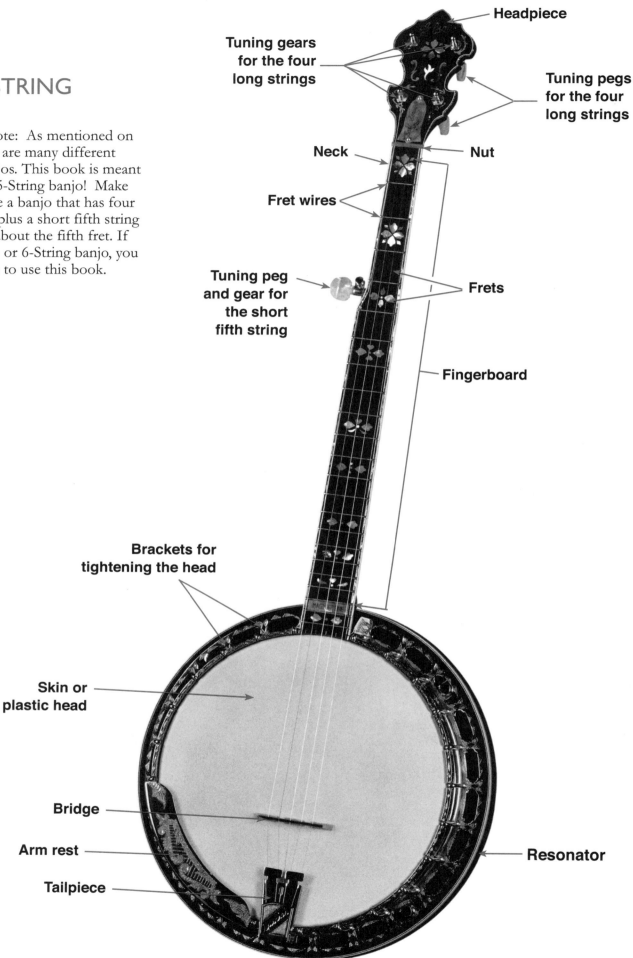

Headpiece

Tuning gears for the four long strings

Tuning pegs for the four long strings

Neck

Nut

Fret wires

Frets

Tuning peg and gear for the short fifth string

Fingerboard

Brackets for tightening the head

Skin or plastic head

Bridge

Arm rest

Resonator

Tailpiece

THE HANDS

The fingers of the left hand are numbered:
4   3   2   1   T

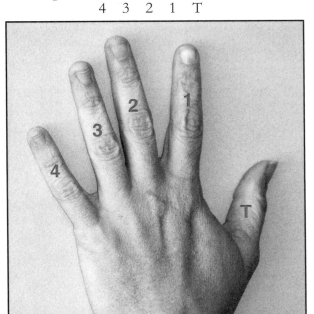

The fingers of the right hand are named:
Thumb   Index   Middle   Ring

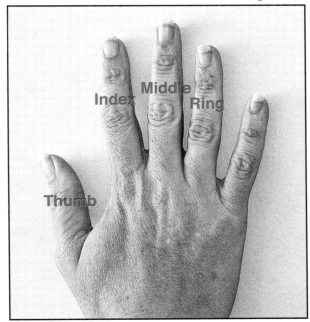

PICKS

For added brightness of tone and speed of execution, picks are sometimes worn on the thumb, index and middle finger of the right hand (see pages 44 and 52).

TIGHTENING THE HEAD

The head should be tightened periodically. In order to do this you'll need a small tool called a bracket wrench (it looks like an old-fashioned skate key). Turn the banjo over and start with the first bracket to the right of the neck. Tighten it (clockwise) about a quarter turn. Skip the next bracket and tighten the third bracket about a quarter turn. Continue all around the banjo in this way, tightening every other bracket. Then go around the banjo again, this time tightening all the brackets you skipped the first time. Then test the head by snapping your fingernail against it. It should sound bright and sharp. If not, do another series of tightenings. However, be careful not to over-tighten the head, as this could cause it to split. (Heads can be replaced at a cost starting at about $15.00 or $20.00.)

GETTING STARTED — HOLDING THE BANJO

If you prefer to play sitting down, we suggest holding the banjo either with both feet flat on the floor or with the left leg crossed over the right.

If you stand when you play the banjo, you'll need a strap to support it. The strap is attached to two brackets on the body of the instrument.

▲ *Sitting with feet flat on the floor*

▲ *Sitting with left leg crossed over right*

▲ *Using a strap to play standing up*

TUNING YOUR BANJO   Track 1

First make sure you understand how each string is wound around the tuning peg. Notice how the four long strings come up between the pegs and are threaded through them. The two highest long strings are wound around the two right-hand pegs in a clockwise direction. The two lowest long strings are wound around the left-hand pegs in a counterclockwise direction. Each peg is controlled by a small plastic handle connected to the **tuning gears**. Turning the handle counterclockwise causes the sound of the string (musicians call this *pitch*) to go higher. Turning the handle clockwise makes the pitch go lower.

The fifth string is also threaded through a tuning peg attached to a tuning handle. Here again, turning the tuning handle counterclockwise raises the pitch; turning the handle clockwise lowers the pitch.

Make sure you understand this before attempting to tune the banjo.

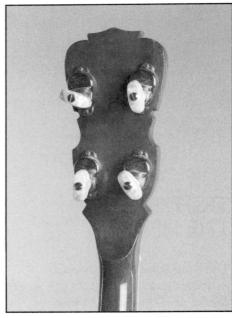

▲ *The banjo's tuning pegs, handles and gears*

Tuning to a Keyboard Instrument

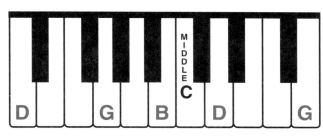

1. Find middle C on the keyboard.

2. Find middle D (this is the white key directly to the right of middle C).

3. Strike middle D and hold it with the pedal (if the keyboard has one). Then tune the first string to this note. (The first string is the one closest to the floor.) Tighten or loosen the string till it sounds like the note on the keyboard.

4. Tighten or loosen the second string until it sounds like the note B below middle C (the white key directly to the left of middle C).

5. Start with middle C. Moving to the left, skip two white keys and play the next white key. This note is G below middle C. Tighten or loosen the third string until it sounds like this note.

6. Starting with the G you just found, move to the left. Skip two white keys and play the next one. This note is D below middle C. Tighten or loosen the fourth string until it sounds like this note.

7. Finally, find the note G above middle C. This note is the fourth white key above middle C. Tighten or loosen the short fifth string until it sounds like this note.

This completes the tuning procedure using a keyboard.

Note: This is called the **G tuning**. Later in this book we'll show you that this isn't the only tuning used on the five-string banjo. It is, however, the easiest and most popular, so we'll start with it.

Tuning to a Pitch Pipe

A pitch pipe doesn't cost much, and if you don't have a keyboard they can be useful for tuning. Make sure to get a pitch pipe on which you can produce all 12 possible notes.

1. Tighten or loosen the first string until it matches the sound of the note D.

2. Tighten or loosen the second string until it matches the note B.

3. Continue in this way and tune the third string to the note G.

4. Tune the fourth string to D an *octave* lower than the first string. (An octave is a musical interval of eight notes. You can remember the sound of an octave by singing the first two notes of the song "Over the Rainbow.")

5. Tune the short fifth string to G an octave above the third string.

Tuning to a Tuning Fork

Make sure you purchase a tuning fork that sounds the note A. This note will be stamped into the fork, usually as "A=440." Strike the fork on something soft like your elbow (never a hard surface like a table). Then place the stem of the fork between your back teeth. You'll hear the note "A" by bone conduction. The advantage of this method is that it leaves both hands free for tuning the banjo.

1. Finger the first string at the seventh fret. This note should match the sound of the fork. If it doesn't, tighten or loosen the string until it does.

2. Release the first string and finger the second string at the third fret. This sound should match the first string played open (that is, without pressing down on a fret).

3. Finger the third string at the fourth fret. Tighten or loosen it until it matches the sound of the open second string.

4. Finger the fourth string at the fifth fret. Tighten or loosen it until it matches the sound of the open third string.

5. Tighten or loosen the short fifth string till it matches the sound of the third string at the 12th fret.

Tuning by Ear

If you have neither keyboard, pitch pipe nor tuning fork, you can tune by ear. Tune the first string as best you can, then follow steps 2, 3, 4 and 5 listed in "Tuning to a Tuning Fork."

Using an Electronic Tuner

An electronic tuner can be purchased at any music store. They range in quality and price, but some of the low-end models can be bought for $40 or less. You pluck the string, and an easy-to-read dial tells you when the string is at the correct pitch.

The advantages of using an electronic tuner are that it's easy and accurate. But relying solely on an electronic tuner can hinder the need for you to train your ear. Anyone who hopes to play reasonably well must depend on the ear to tell when something is correct or not and, more subtly, to tell whether a tune is being played tastefully or not.

Suggestion: Tune the instrument using one of the methods described above. Then check the tuning using the electronic tuner.

CARING FOR YOUR BANJO

Strings should be wiped with a soft rag after each session of playing, otherwise they start to corrode from the dampness and lose their brilliance. With ordinary usage strings should last for about three months. After that it's time to put on a new set.

It's best to ask your local music dealer to string your banjo. If you decide to do it yourself, replace one string at a time, and bring each new string up to pitch before replacing the next one. This is important! If you remove all the strings at once, the bridge will slip out of place and it's no small job to get it reset properly.

Once a week or so wipe down the wooden parts of the banjo with a light polish such as the kind guitar players use. This will not only keep the instrument looking nice, but will protect the surfaces against dust and dirt. The plastic head can be cleaned using a damp cloth. But make sure you squeeze all the excess moisture out of the cloth, as excess moisture can damage the head.

About every six months put a tiny drop of sewing machine oil (or some other very light oil) in the tuning gears to lubricate them and keep them from rusting.

Above all, protect the banjo from extremes of heat or cold. If you live in a cold climate, don't leave the instrument in your car overnight. Also, it's not a good idea to leave your banjo in your car during warm days.

It's best to have a hard case for the banjo to protect it when it's not being played. The neck and head of the instrument are especially vulnerable. Never lean the banjo against a wall or a chair where the neck may get broken. Although the entire neck can be replaced (for a substantial amount of money), it's virtually impossible to repair a broken neck successfully. If you can't afford a hard case, a cardboard case is your next best option. The least safe option is a padded leather or vinyl bag commonly called a "gig bag." Although convenient and easy to carry, the gig bag provides little protection for the neck and head of the banjo. Gig bags should only be used in very controlled situations such as taking your banjo from the car to the bandstand.

BUYING A USED BANJO

A first-rate, new banjo can sell for thousands of dollars. So unless you find an old one in Uncle Oscar's closet, you may want to buy a used instrument. If you do, here are a few things to look for:

1. *Is the neck straight?* Look for bowing from end to end or twisting from side to side. Either of these imperfections are cause for immediately rejecting the instrument.

2. *Can the tuning gears be turned fairly easily?* They may only need a little oil. But if they are bent or rusted, be prepared to spend up to $100 to have them replaced. Unless you've found a real collector's item, it may not be worthwhile replacing the tuning gears.

3. *Is the neck crack-free?* If you see that the neck has been broken and then repaired, reject the instrument. It will probably give you nothing but trouble. However, small cracks in the resonator will probably not affect the tone.

4. *Is the action fairly easy?* (The word "action" refers to how high off of the fingerboard the strings are.) You should be able to slide a shirt cardboard between the strings and the fingerboard, but if the strings are any further away than this they will be difficult to push down and will hurt your fingers. Any competent repair person will be able to adjust the action if the instrument has nothing else wrong with it.

5. *Is the head undamaged?* If the plastic head has split or has a hole in it, it must be replaced. (Since replacing a banjo head costs only about $15 or $20, it's not reason enough to reject the instrument.)

Sonny Osborne (here with his band The Obsorne Brothers) is noted for a style that encompasses simple bluegrass, folk and mainstream country. The band's most famous song, *Rocky Top,* became the Tennessee state song. *Photo courtesy of Country Music Foundation.*

STARTING TO PLAY CHORDS

The banjo is a wonderful instrument for playing chords. A **chord** is a group of three or more notes which sound good together. Chords are used to accompany singing or another instrument or to add to the total sound of a musical group.

Playing the G Chord

The easiest chord to play on the 5-String banjo is the G chord. In a single, rapid downward motion strike all five open strings with the fingernails of your right hand. Strike the strings about halfway between the bridge and the end of the neck.

▲ *The right hand before striking the strings*

▲ *The right hand after striking the strings*

This book uses diagrams to indicate fingerings. Notice that the diagram only has four strings. This is because the short fifth string is never fingered, so there is no need for it to appear on the diagram. Here's what the diagram looks like when no left-hand fingers are being used:

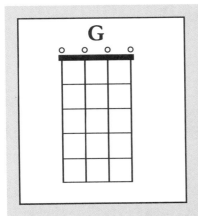

The **large capital G** means that this diagram is for the G major chord.

The **vertical lines** represent the four long strings.

The **horizontal lines** represent the frets. The highest horizontal line is thicker because it represents the nut.

An "o" above a vertical line means the that string is played **open** (without using any left-hand fingers).

PLAYING THE G CHORD (continued)

When chords are used for accompanying a singer or instrumentalist, symbols and slash marks (/) are used to tell you which chord to play and how many times to play it. For example, **G / / /**

means to play the G chord four times; once for the G and once for each of the slash marks.

In many songs chords are played in groups of three called **three-quarter** or **three-four time**.

Look for the time signature $\frac{3}{4}$ at the beginning of the piece. In the exercise below, the vertical lines are called **bar lines**. They mark the end of each group of three.

Track 2

1. $\frac{3}{4}$ G / / | G / / | G / / | G / / | G / / | G / / | G / / | G / / ‖

Play each G chord by striking down on the strings with the fingernails of the right hand. The left hand does nothing except hold the instrument. Stress the first chord of each group of three. Count: **one** two three, **one** two three, etc.

Another common grouping for chords is called **four-quarter** or **four-four time**. Look for the time signature $\frac{4}{4}$ at the beginning of the piece. Each group of four beats is called a **measure**. Stress the first chord in each measure. Count: **one** two three four, **one** two three four, etc.

Track 3

2. $\frac{4}{4}$ G / / / | G / / / | G / / / | G / / / | G / / / | G / / / | G / / / | G / / / ‖

Practice the above exercises in $\frac{3}{4}$ and $\frac{4}{4}$ time until you feel comfortable strumming at slow, medium and fast speeds or *tempos*. (Tempo is an Italian word used to indicate how fast music is to be played.) Whichever tempo you choose, keep the beat steady throughout the exercise.

Note: You may want to buy a **metronome**, which is an invaluable device that can be set to "click" at any tempo between 40 or 240 beats per minute. Using a metronome is a great way to discipline yourself in keeping a steady tempo.

Bela Fleck (pictured here with the New Grass Revival) combines both traditional bluegrass with jazz and classical music, creating an eclectic and expansive style.

Photo courtesy of Country Music Foundation.

Playing the D7 Chord

Of course, banjo playing would get pretty dull if all you did was strum the G chord. So the next thing we'll do is learn how to play another chord, the D7 chord. You'll use two fingers on the left hand to play it. Here's a picture and a diagram.

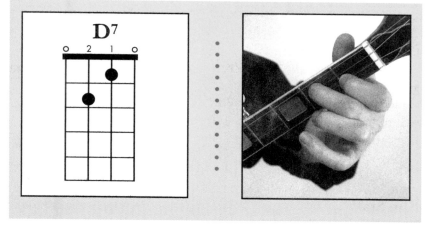

Make sure your fingers press down firmly just to the left of (not directly on!) each fret. Test the strings individually to make sure that each one sounds clear—no buzzes or dull thunks. Once you can play the D7 clearly, practice strumming it at different tempos.

 Track 4

1. (sheet music) 3/4 D7 / / | D7 / / | D7 / / | D7 / / | D7 / / | D7 / / | D7 / / | D7 / / ‖

 Track 5

2. (sheet music) 4/4 D7 / / / | D7 / / / | D7 / / / | D7 / / / | D7 / / / | D7 / / / | D7 / / / | D7 / / / ‖

Since even the simplest song usually requires at least two chords to accompany it, the ability to change from one chord to another without hesitation or missing a beat is of the greatest importance. The following exercises require that you change from G to D7 and back again. Practice these exercises very slowly at first. It's important to change chords smoothly and without hesitation. Once you can make the changes at a very slow tempo, gradually get faster. If you have a metronome, start at about 40 clicks per minute and gradually work your way up to about a marching beat (120 clicks per minute).

 Track 6

1. (sheet music) 4/4 G / / / | G / / / | D7 / / / | D7 / / / | G / / / | G / / / | D7 / / / | G / / / ‖

 Track 7

2. (sheet music) 3/4 G / / | G / / | D7 / / | D7 / / | G / / | G / / | D7 / / | D7 / / | G / / | G (strum and hold) ‖

 Track 8

3. (sheet music) 4/4 G / / / | D7 / / / | G / / / | D7 / / / | G / / / | D7 / / / | G / / / | G (strum and hold) ‖

 Track 9

4. (sheet music) 4/4 G / D7 / | G / D7 / | G / D7 / | G / D7 / | G / D7 / | G (strum and hold) ‖

GETTING ACQUAINTED WITH MUSIC

Notes

Musical sounds are indicated by symbols called NOTES. Their time value is determined by their color (white or black) and by stems and flags attached to the note.

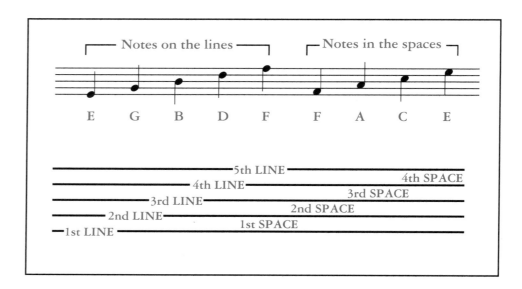

Whole notes look like:	Dotted half notes look like	Half notes look like:	Quarter notes look like:
o	𝅗𝅥. or 𝅗𝅥•	𝅗𝅥 or 𝅗𝅥	𝅘𝅥 or 𝅘𝅥
They last for four beats.	They last for three beats.	They last for two beats.	They last for one beat.

The Staff

The name and pitch of the notes are determined by the note's position on five horizontal lines and the spaces in between, called the STAFF. The notes are named after the first seven letters of the alphabet (A–G), repeated to embrace the entire range of musical sound.

Notes on the lines — Notes in the spaces

E   G   B   D   F   F   A   C   E

5th LINE
4th LINE   4th SPACE
3rd LINE   3rd SPACE
2nd LINE   2nd SPACE
1st SPACE
1st LINE

Measures and Bar Lines

Music is also divided into equal parts, called MEASURES. One measure is divided from another by a BAR LINE.

BAR LINES

←MEASURE→ ←MEASURE→

Clefs

During the evolution of music notation, the staff had from two to twenty lines, and symbols were invented to locate a reference line, or pitch, by which all other pitches were determined. These symbols were called CLEFS.

Music for the banjo is written in the G or treble clef. Originally the Gothic letter G was used on a four-line staff to establish the pitch of G:

This developed into the modern clef:

G

Flats ♭, Sharps ♯ and Naturals ♮

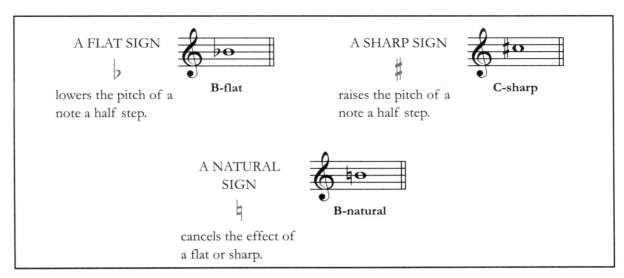

Key Signatures

To make the writing process easier, we can indicate the flats or sharps to be used in a composition at the beginning of the piece. This is called a **key signature** and tells the performer that the accidentals (flats and sharps) indicated are in effect throughout the piece.

For example the F♯ in this key signature, which appears on the top line of the staff immediately following the clef, indicates that all of the F's in this composition are to be played F♯.

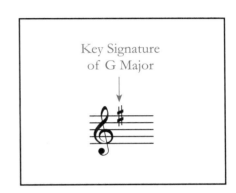

Rests

A rest is a measured silence that lasts for a certain number of beats. Remember these three:

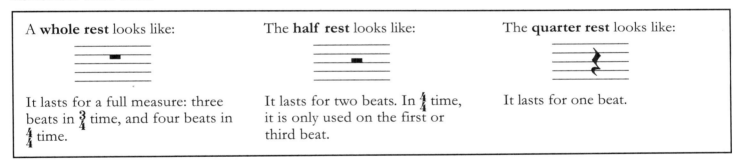

A **whole rest** looks like:

It lasts for a full measure: three beats in ¾ time, and four beats in ¼ time.

The **half rest** looks like:

It lasts for two beats. In ⁴⁄₄ time, it is only used on the first or third beat.

The **quarter rest** looks like:

It lasts for one beat.

Special Notation

In this book you'll find a fraction below every melody note. The upper number of the fraction tells you the string on which the note is found. The lower number tells you which fret to play. In this way you can pick out tunes without reading music.

Track 10

MINI MUSIC LESSON

TIES

This curved line is called a **tie**. It connects two or more notes and ties them together. Play or sing the note once and hold it for the value of both (or more) tied notes.

The chords used in this song are:

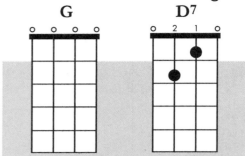

Down in the Valley

Track 11

Key Signature: remember to play all F's a ½ step higher, F♯.

Moderately

American Folk Song

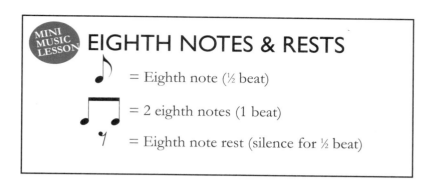

EIGHTH NOTES & RESTS

♪ = Eighth note (½ beat)

♫ = 2 eighth notes (1 beat)

♪ = Eighth note rest (silence for ½ beat)

The chords used in this song are:

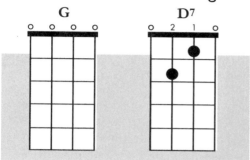

Go Tell Aunt Rhody Track 12

Moderately

American Folk Song

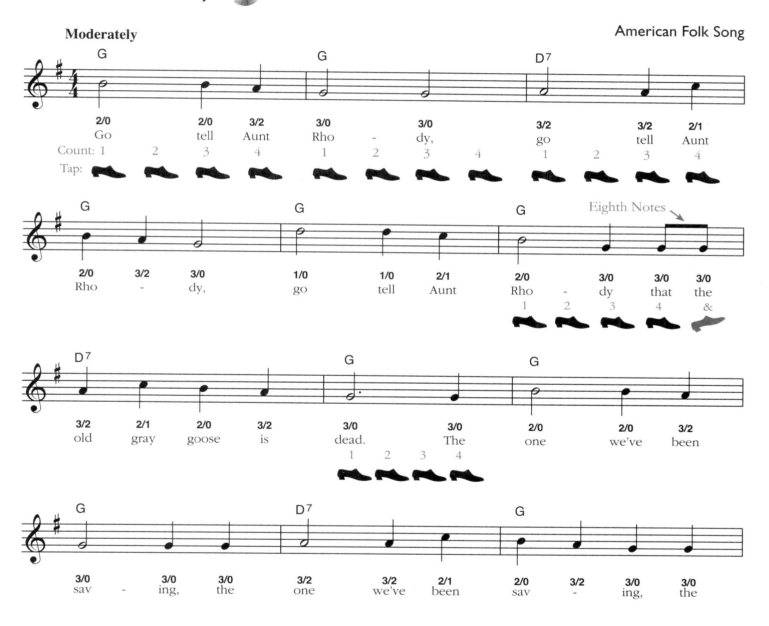

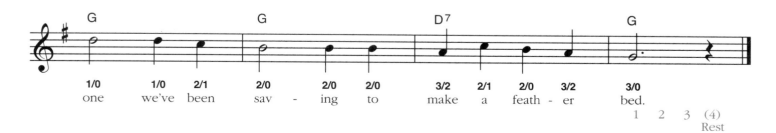

PICKUP MEASURES

Sometimes a song begins with an incomplete measure called a **pickup**. The pickup measure contains fewer beats than are called for in the time signature. For example, a $\frac{3}{4}$ measure may contain one or two beats. Often (but not always) the last measure of the piece will be missing the same number of beats that the pickup uses. In this way the initial incomplete measure is completed.

Look at the last measure of *Cockles and Mussels*. It has only two beats. These two beats, plus the one beat in the pickup measure (the first measure), complete one measure of $\frac{3}{4}$ time.

DOTTED QUARTER NOTE

A dotted quarter note equals 1½ beats.

Count: 1 (& 2) &
Tap:

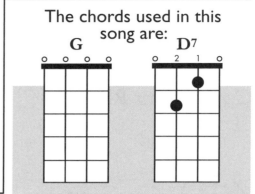

The chords used in this song are:

G   D7

Cockles and Mussels

Track 13

Moderately

Irish Folk Melody

The chords used in this song are:

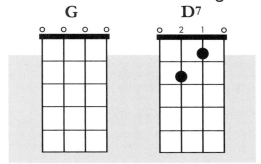

Clementine

 Track 14

American Folk Song

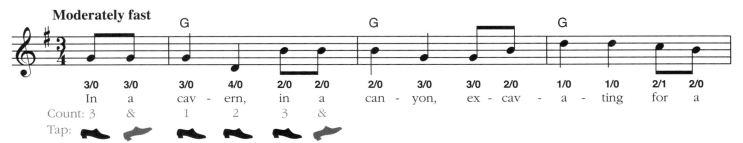

In a cav - ern, in a can - yon, ex - cav - a - ting for a

Count: 3 & 1 2 3 &

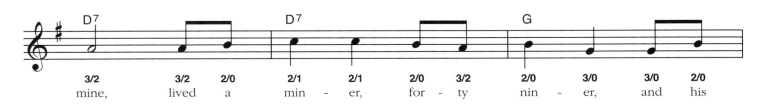

mine, lived a min - er, for - ty nin - er, and his

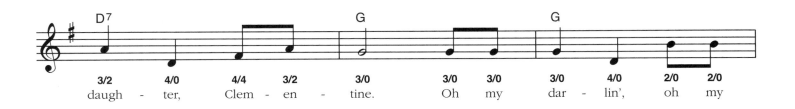

daugh - ter, Clem - en - tine. Oh my dar - lin', oh my

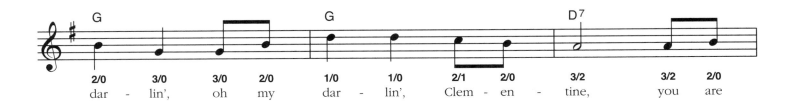

dar - lin', oh my dar - lin', Clem - en - tine, you are

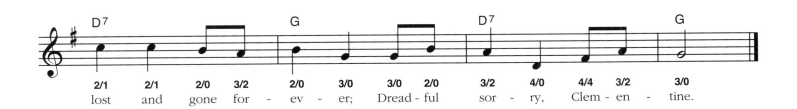

lost and gone for - ev - er; Dread - ful sor - ry, Clem - en - tine.

By now you should be comfortable singing while keeping a steady beat on the banjo by strumming the G and D7 chords. So far we have used the word "strum" as a verb meaning "to strike down across the strings." When strum is used as a noun, it is the name of a particular rhythmic pattern used to accompany a song.

STRUM NO. 1

Strum No. 1 is very effective when used to accompany songs in $\frac{4}{4}$ time at moderate to fast tempos. Here's how it's done:

1st beat
Using the fingernail of the right-hand index finger, pull up (toward your face) on any long string.

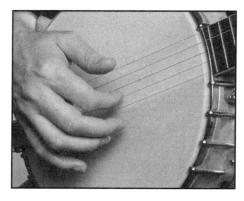

2nd beat
Strum down across all the strings with the fingernails of the right hand.

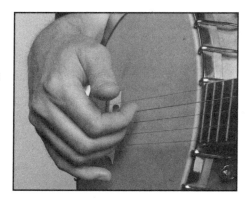

3rd beat
Using the fingernail of the right-hand index finger, pull up on any long string. Aim for a string different from the one you played on the first beat.

4th beat
Strum down across the strings as on the second beat.

Summing up, this means that each measure of $\frac{4}{4}$ time is played:

1	2	3	4
Pick up with index finger	Strum down	Pick up with index finger	Strum down

Try this pattern on the open G chord. Keep doing it until you can play it smoothly, almost without thinking.

Now switch to the D7 chord and keep playing Strum No. 1.

Now switch back and forth between the G chord and the D7 chord. Play one complete strum on each chord and then switch. Guess what? You're starting to sound like a banjo player!

Once you can do Strum No. 1 on both the G and D7 chords without hesitating or missing a beat, go back to "Go Tell Aunt Rhody" on page 15 and play it using Strum No. 1. Then try "Tom Dooley" on page 19.

D.C. AL FINE

D.C. al Fine stands for *Da Capo al Fine* (Dah cah-po al Fee-nay), which is a musical term of Italian origin. It means to go back to the beginning of the piece and play through to the word *Fine*. At the end of this particular piece, return to the beginning then stop at the end of the second line.

The chords used in this song are:

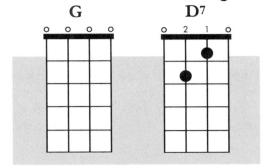

Tom Dooley Track 15

Words and music collected, adapted
and arranged by Frank Warner, John A.
Lomax and Alan Lomax

From the singing of Frank Proffitt

American Folk Song

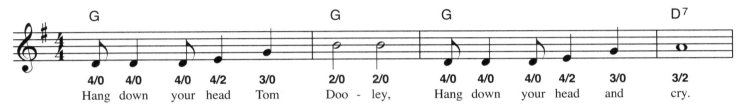

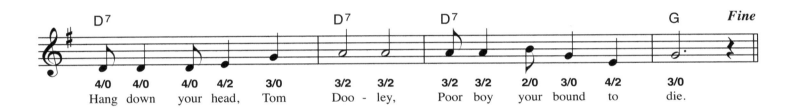

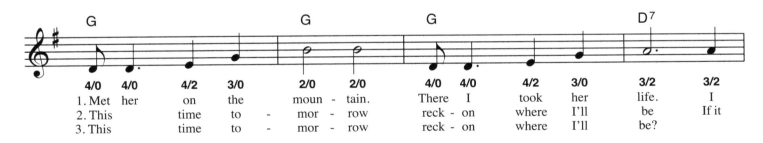

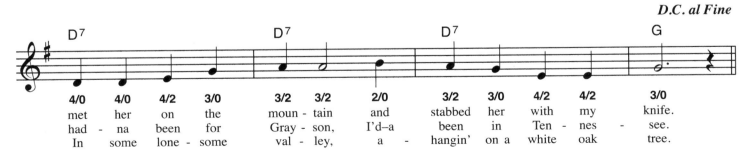

STRUM NO. 2

Strum No. 2 is used to accompany moderate to fast songs in ¾ time. It is similar to Strum No. 1.

1st beat	2nd beat	3rd beat
Using the fingernail of the right-hand index finger, pull up on any long string.	Strum down across the strings with the fingernails of the right hand.	Same as the second beat.

This means that each measure of ¾ time is played:

1	2	3
Pick up with index finger	Strum down	Strum down

Once you can do Strum No. 2 on the G and D7 chords, go back to pages 14, 16 and 17 and use this strum to accompany "Down in the Valley," "Cockles and Mussels" and "Clementine." Then try the next tune, "Old Paint."

The chords used in this song are:

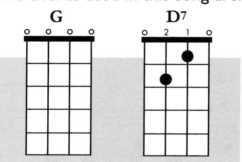

Old Paint Track 16

American Cowboy Song

Additional Verse:

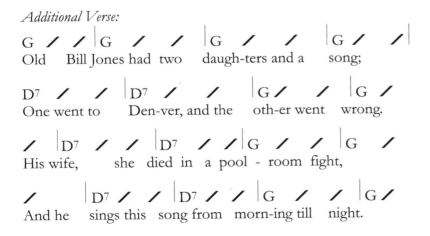

G / / | G / / | G / / | G / / |
Old Bill Jones had two daugh-ters and a song;

D7 / / | D7 / / | G / / | G / |
One went to Den-ver, and the oth-er went wrong.

/ | D7 / / | D7 / / | G / / | G / |
His wife, she died in a pool - room fight,

/ | D7 / / | D7 / / | G / / | G / |
And he sings this song from morn-ing till night.

(Repeat Chorus)

The C Major Chord

The C chord, along with the G and D7 chords you have learned, comprise a group of three chords called the **principal chords** in the key of G. Using only these three chords you can accompany literally thousands of folk, country, blues and other songs.

If a chord symbol does not have "7," "min." or some other abbreviation after it, it is always a **major** chord. Thus G and C are both major chords. Here's how to play the C major chord:

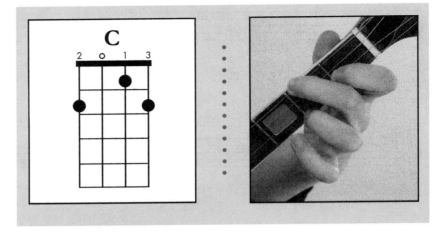

Finger the C chord as shown above. Then play the strings one at a time to make each one sound clear. No buzzes or dull thunks, please! Once you can play the C chord perfectly, practice the first exercise in $\frac{4}{4}$ using Strum No. 1. Then use Strum No. 2 to play the second exercise.

Track 17

Track 18

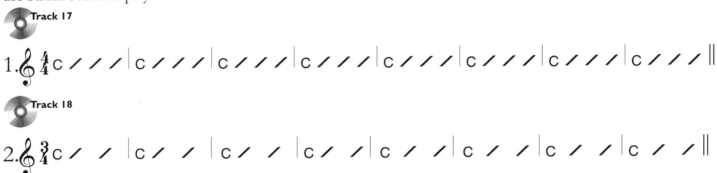

The following exercises will train your fingers to change chords smoothly. Keep a steady beat. This is very important. If you have a metronome, set it at 60 beats per minute and play through the exercises using the basic strum (striking down on the strings with the fingernails of the right hand). When you can do this smoothly, without hesitating or missing a beat, gradually increase the tempo until you can play the exercises at 120 beats per minute (marching beat).

Track 19

Track 20

Track 21

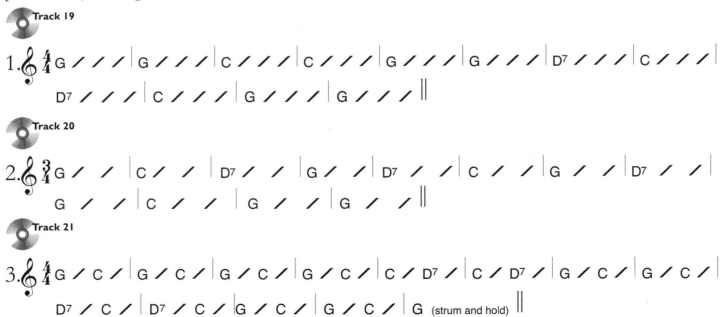

After you can play the above exercises using the basic strum, try the two exercises in $\frac{4}{4}$ using Strum No. 1 and the exercise in $\frac{3}{4}$ using Strum No. 2.

The chords used in this song are:

In this arrangement you'll start by strumming four measures as an introduction. This serves the purpose of setting the tempo and getting the key fixed in your mind before you start singing. Once you can play the song using the basic strum, try it with Strum No. 1.

When the Saints Go Marching In Track 22

Gospel and Dixieland Jazz Standard

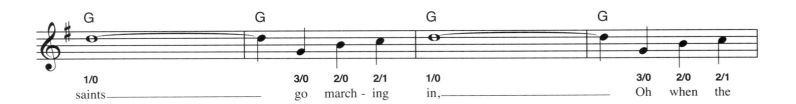

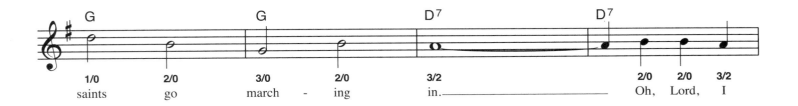

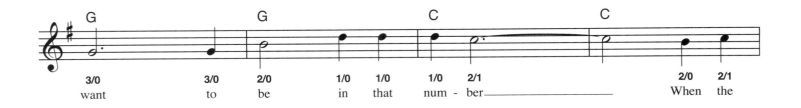

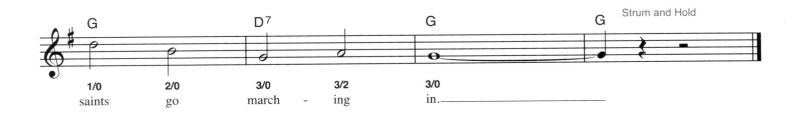

Use either the basic strum or Strum No. 2 to play this country favorite.

On Top of Old Smokey Track 23

The chords used in this song are:

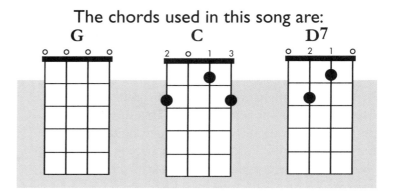

Appalachian Folk Song

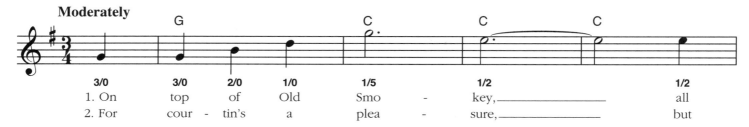

1. On top of Old Smo - key,_____ all
2. For cour - tin's a plea - sure,_____ but

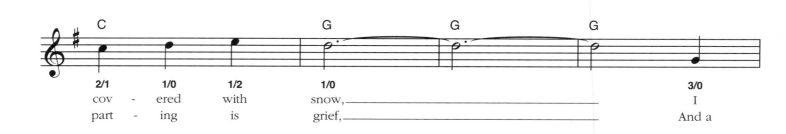

cov - ered with snow,_____ I
part - ing is grief,_____ And a

lost my true lov - er_____ from
false - heart - ed lov - er_____ is

Strum and hold

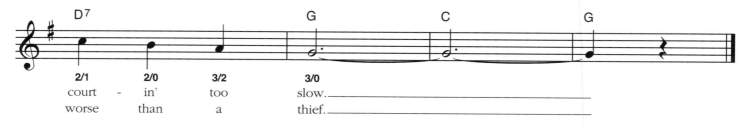

court - in' too slow._____
worse than a thief._____

The chords used in this song are:

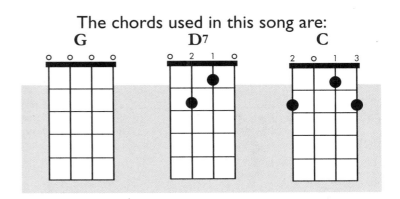

What would a banjo book be without this classic? Use either the basic strum or Strum No. 1 to accompany it.

Oh! Susanna

 Track 24

Stephen Foster

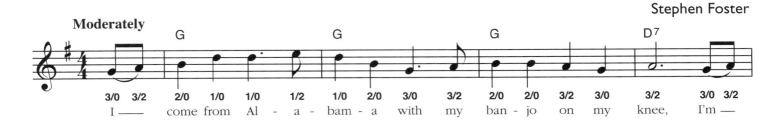

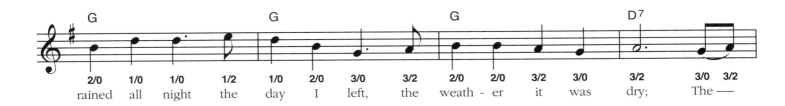

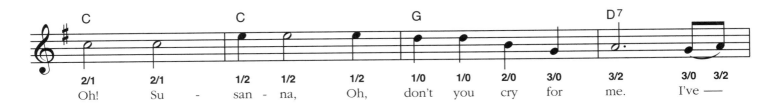

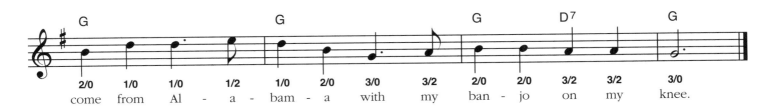

STRUM NO. 3

This strum is used for moderately-fast to fast songs in $\frac{4}{4}$ time. It gets a similar sound to Strum No. 1, but can be played at a faster tempo. It will also train your right-hand fingers in preparation for more advanced strums and, eventually, bluegrass picking styles. Here's how to do it:

1st beat

Pick up with the index finger of the right hand on any long string.

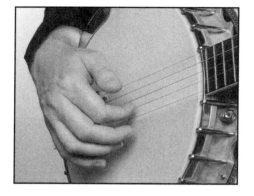

2nd beat

Brush down across the strings with the fingernail of the right-hand middle finger.

3rd beat

Pick up with the index finger of the right hand on any long string. Try to play a different string than you did on the first beat.

4th beat

Brush down across the strings with the fingernail of the right-hand middle finger exactly as you did on the second beat.

Summing up, this means that each measure of $\frac{4}{4}$ time is played:

1. Pick up with index finger
2. Brush down with middle finger
3. Pick up with index finger
4. Brush down with middle finger

STRUM NO. 4

Strum No. 4 is an adaptation of Strum No. 3 to be used with songs in $\frac{3}{4}$. Here's how to do it:

1st beat

Pick up with the index finger of the right hand on any long string.

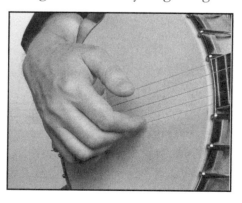

2nd beat

Brush down with the fingernail of the right-hand middle finger.

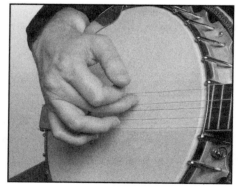

3rd beat

Same as second beat

Summing up, this means that every measure of $\frac{3}{4}$ time is played:

1. Pick up with index finger
2. Brush down with middle finger
3. Brush down with middle finger

Suggestion: Practice the new strums on the open G chord until you can play them smoothly. Then practice them on the D7 and C chords. Finally, go back to all the songs you have learned and play them using Strum No. 3 for those in $\frac{4}{4}$ and Strum No. 4 for those in $\frac{3}{4}$.

The chords used in this song are:

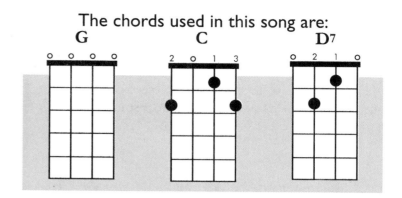

You can use the basic strum, Strum No. 1 or Strum No. 3 to accompany this great old blues song. Better yet, use a different strum for each verse.

Worried Man Blues Track 25

American Folk Song

Moderately, with a beat

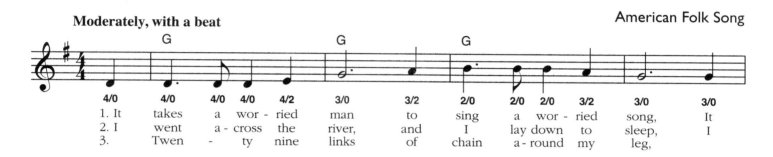

1. It takes a wor - ried man to sing a wor - ried song, It
2. I went a - cross the river, and I lay down to sleep, I
3. Twen - ty nine links of chain a - round my leg,

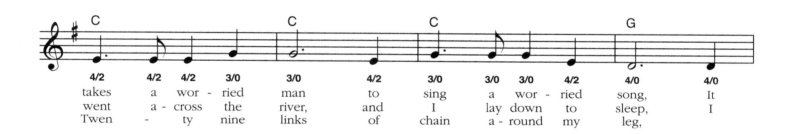

takes a wor - ried man to sing a wor - ried song, It
went a - cross the river, and I lay down to sleep, I
Twen - ty nine links of chain a - round my leg,

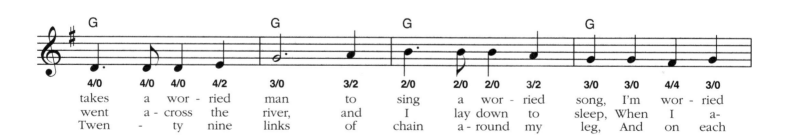

takes a wor - ried man to sing a wor - ried song, I'm wor - ried
went a - cross the river, and I lay down to sleep, When I a -
Twen - ty nine links of chain a - round my leg, And on each

Strum and hold
(last time only)

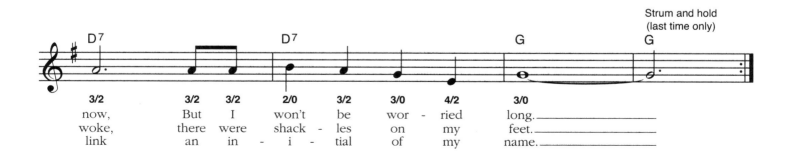

now, But I won't be wor - ried long._____
woke, there were shack - les on my feet._____
link an in - i - tial of my name._____

The G7 Chord

As you have already learned (on page 22), the G, C and D7 chords are the principal chords in the key of G. The G7 chord is also often used in this key as a sort of "color" chord, especially in blues songs. Here's how to play it:

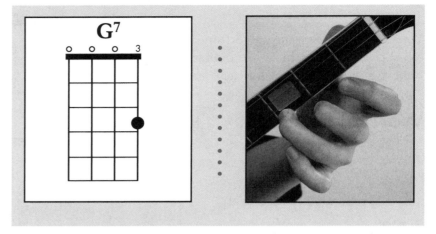

Practice the following exercises to get the G7 chord under your fingers. Once you can play the exercises without hesitation, try the next few songs using whatever strum you think appropriate.

Track 26

1. $\frac{4}{4}$ G / / / | G / / / | G / / / | G7 / / / | C / / / | C / / / | G / / / | G / / / |

   D7 / / / | C / / / | G / / / | G / / / ‖

Track 27

2. $\frac{3}{4}$ G / / | D7 / / | G / / | G / / | C / / | G7 / / | C / / | C / / |

   G / / | D7 / / | G / / | G / / ‖

Track 28

3. $\frac{4}{4}$ G / C / | G7 / C / | G / C / | G7 / C / | G / C / | G7 / C / | G / / / | G / / / ‖

The chords used in this song are:

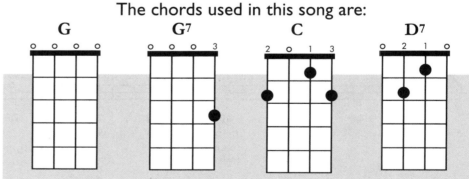

Jesse James   **Track 29**

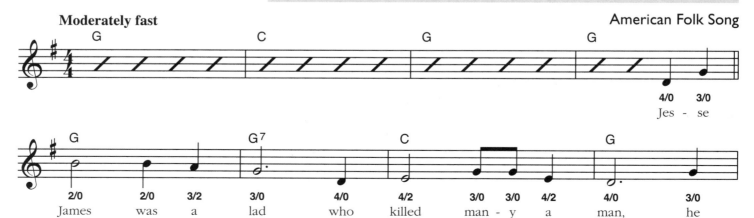

Moderately fast   **American Folk Song**

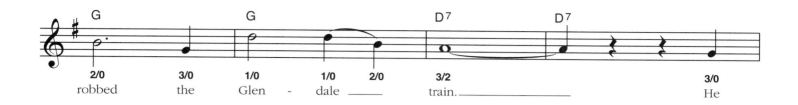

2/0 robbed   3/0 the   1/0 Glen - 1/0 dale   2/0   3/2 train.   3/0 He

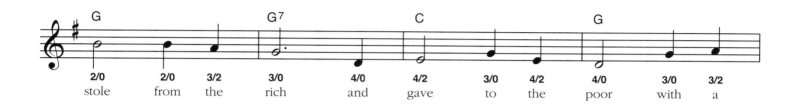

2/0 stole   2/0 from   3/2 the   3/0 rich   4/0 and   4/2 gave   3/0 to   4/2 the   4/0 poor   3/0 with   3/2 a

2/0 hand   2/0 and   2/0 a   3/2 heart   3/2 and   3/2 a   3/0 brain.   3/0 Poor

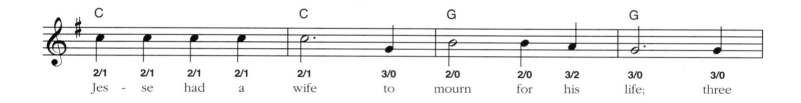

2/1 Jes - 2/1 se 2/1 had 2/1 a 2/1 wife   3/0 to   2/0 mourn   2/0 for   3/2 his   3/0 life;   3/0 three

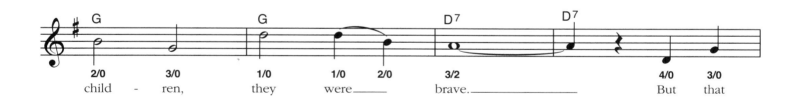

2/0 child - 3/0 ren,   1/0 they   1/0 were 2/0   3/2 brave.   4/0 But   3/0 that

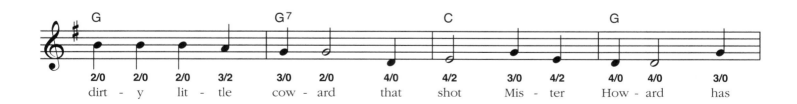

2/0 dirt - 2/0 y 2/0 lit - 3/2 tle   3/0 cow - 2/0 ard   4/0 that   4/2 shot   3/0 Mis - 4/2 ter   4/0 How - 4/0 ard   3/0 has

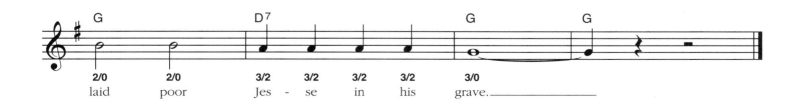

2/0 laid   2/0 poor   3/2 Jes - 3/2 se 3/2 in 3/2 his   3/0 grave.

She'll Be Comin' 'Round the Mountain

Track 30

Brightly

American Folk Song

(continue similarly)

2. She'll be ridin' six white horses when she comes...

3. She'll be wearin' silk pajamas when she comes...

4. Oh, we'll all go out to meet her when she comes...

* This note played an *8va* higher.

The chords used in this song are:

Red River Valley — Track 31

Canadian/American Folk Song

STRUM NO. 5

This is a strum used on moderate to fast songs in $\frac{4}{4}$ time. Years ago it was popularized through the playing of a master of the folk banjo, Pete Seeger.

Unlike the other strums you've learned so far, this strum has different rhythms in it. Before attempting it, practice counting from one to four, subdividing each beat by saying "*one* and *two* and *three*

and *four* and." If you're tapping your foot, tap down on the numbers; on the "ands" your foot is up. Now, here's how to do the actual strum:

1st beat

1st beat Pick up on any long string using the index finger of the right hand.

and

Do nothing

2nd beat

Strum down on the long strings using the middle finger of the right hand.

and

Pick down on the 5th string (the short string) using the right-hand thumb.

3rd beat

Pick up on any other long string using the right-hand index finger.

and

Do nothing

4th beat

Strum down with the middle finger of the right hand.

and

Pick down on the 5th string with the thumb.

1	and	2	and	3	and	4	and
Pick up on any long string		Strum down on long strings	Pick down on short string	Pick up on any long string		Strum down on long strings	Pick down on short string

Start practicing this strum slowly on the open G chord. If you have a metronome, set it at 60 and keep playing playing the strum at that tempo until you get the

coordination down. Then gradually increase the tempo until you can do it at 120 (marching tempo) or even faster. Once you've got the strum working pretty well, practice it on

the exercises below which make use of the four chords you know.

Track 32

1. $\frac{4}{4}$ G / / / | G / / / | C / / / | C / / / | G / / / | G / / / | D7 / / / | D7 / / / | G / / / | G / / / ‖

Track 33

2. $\frac{4}{4}$ G7 / / / | C / / / | G7 / / / | C / / / | D7 / / / | G / / / | D7 / / / | G / / / ‖

Track 34

3. $\frac{4}{4}$ G / / / | G7 / / / | C / / / | G / / / | D7 / / / | C / / / | D7 / / / | G / / / ‖

Many folk songs are written in $\frac{2}{4}$ time. This means that the quarter note gets one beat, and that there are two beats in each measure. Strum No. 5 easily adapts to $\frac{2}{4}$ time. Play the strum exactly the same as in $\frac{4}{4}$, but count it like this:

1	and uh	2	and uh	1	and uh	2	and uh

Keep in mind that the amount of time given the number is the same as for the "and uh."

This hoedown favorite works well with Strum No. 5. Because it is in $\frac{2}{4}$, count it as you learned at the bottom of the previous page.

Skip to My Lou Track 35

The chords used in this song are:

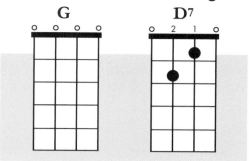

American Square Dance Song

Brightly

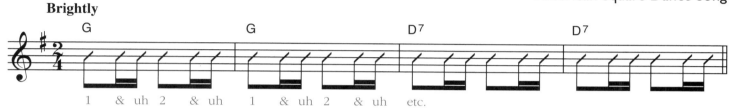

1 & uh 2 & uh   1 & uh 2 & uh   etc.

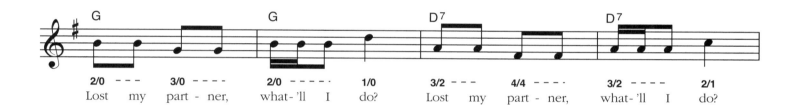

2/0 – – –   3/0 – – – –   2/0 – – – – – ·   1/0   3/2 – – –   4/4 – – – –   3/2 – – – –   2/1
Lost my part - ner,   what-'ll I do?   Lost my part - ner,   what-'ll I do?

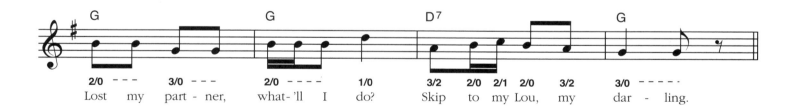

2/0 – – –   3/0 – – –   2/0 – – – –   1/0   3/2 2/0 2/1 2/0 3/2   3/0 – – – – –
Lost my part - ner,   what-'ll I do?   Skip to my Lou, my   dar - ling.

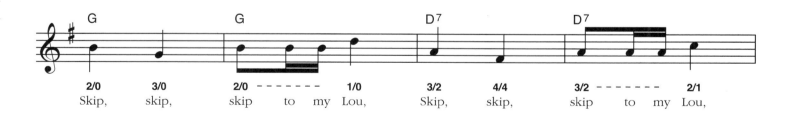

2/0   3/0   2/0 – – – – – –   1/0   3/2   4/4   3/2 – – – – – –   2/1
Skip,   skip,   skip to my Lou,   Skip,   skip,   skip to my Lou,

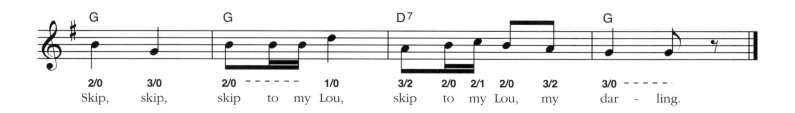

2/0   3/0   2/0 – – – – – –   1/0   3/2 2/0 2/1 2/0 3/2   3/0 – – – – –
Skip,   skip,   skip to my Lou,   skip to my Lou, my   dar - ling.

STRUM NO. 5 (con't)

Strum No. 5 also adapts to songs in **cut time**. The time signature for cut time is **¢**. In cut time there are four beats to the measure, but they are counted in two; that is, each half note gets one beat. Play Strum No. 5 as usual, and count "1 and uh 2 and uh."

The chords used in this song are:

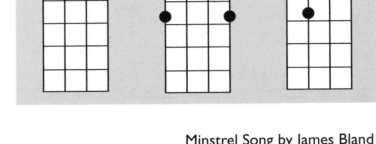

Hand Me Down My Walkin' Cane

Track 36

Minstrel Song by James Bland

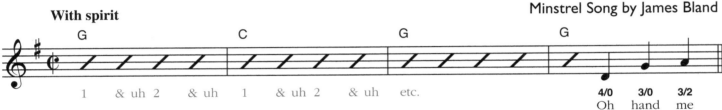

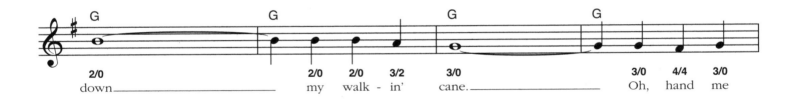

The chords used in this song are:

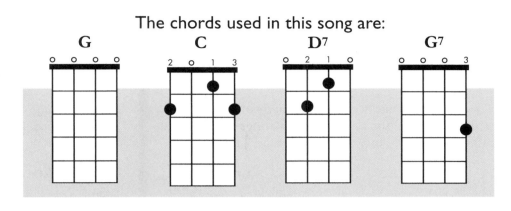

This folk classic is a perfect song on which to play Strum No. 5. Play it with good spirit and a solid beat.

This Land Is Your Land

Track 37

Words and Music by Woody Guthrie

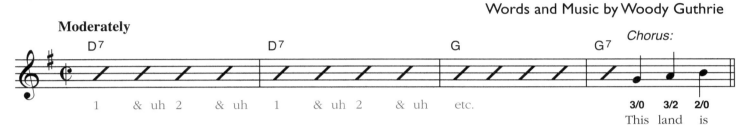

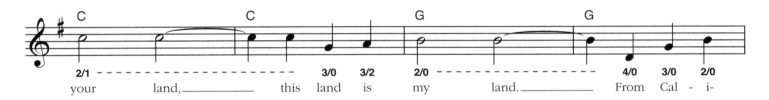

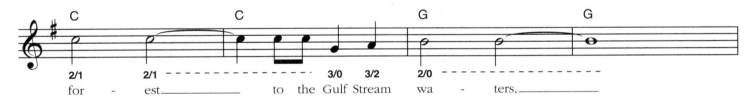

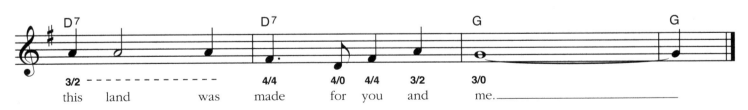

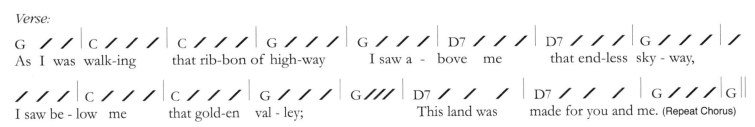

THE ARPEGGIO
Strum No. 6

This type of strum is called an **arpeggio** (ar-*ped*-joe) strum. It is used for accompanying songs in slow to moderate tempos in $\frac{2}{4}$ or, more usually, $\frac{4}{4}$ time.

In $\frac{2}{4}$ time count 1-e-and-a 2-e-and-a. In $\frac{4}{4}$ count "*one* and *two* and *three* and *four* and." Here's what you do on each:

1st beat	2nd beat	3rd beat	4th beat
Thumb picks down on fifth string.	Middle finger picks up on second string.	Thumb picks down on fourth string.	Middle finger picks up on second string.
and	**and**	**and**	**and**
Index picks up on third string.	Ring finger picks up on first string.	Index picks up on third string.	Ring finger picks up on first string.

Summing up, the four beats in a measure of $\frac{4}{4}$ time, or the two beats in a measure of $\frac{2}{4}$, time are played:

In $\frac{4}{4}$ time: In $\frac{2}{4}$ time:	**1** **1**	**and** **uh**	**2** **and**	**and** **uh**	**3** **2**	**and** **uh**	**4** **and**	**and** **uh**
	Thumb picks down on fifth string	Index picks up on third string	Middle picks up on second string	Ring picks up on first string	Thumb picks down on fourth string	Index picks up on third string	Middle picks up on second string	Ring picks up on first string

As usual, practice slowly on the open G chord until the coordination comes easily. Then practice on the other chords and gradually pick up the tempo.

The A⁷ Chord

This chord requires a new fingering technique called the **barre** or, as it's also spelled, **bar**. When using a bar, one finger holds down more than one string. If the finger holds down two or three strings, it's called a **partial bar**. If the finger holds down all four strings it's called a **full bar**. The A7 chord requires the use of a full bar. As you can see from the picture, simply lay the first finger of the left hand directly across the second fret. Pick the strings individually to make sure each one sounds clear. That's all there is to it!

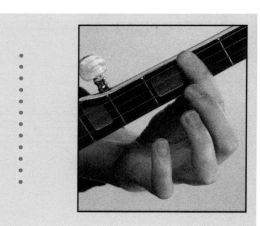

The chords used in this song are:

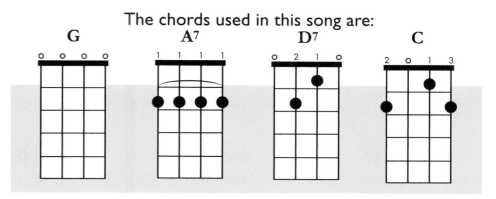

Strum No. 6 is perfect for accompanying this beautiful Civil War ballad. (Elvis Presley did a version of this melody and called it "Love Me Tender.") Use the first four measures as an introduction to set the tempo, mood and key. Then sing the song while playing Strum No. 6.

Aura Lee Track 38

Geo. Poulton and W. W. Fosdick

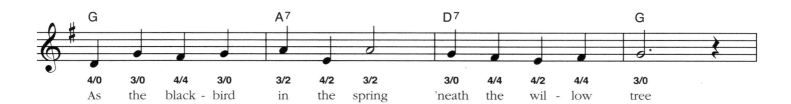

As the black-bird in the spring 'neath the wil-low tree

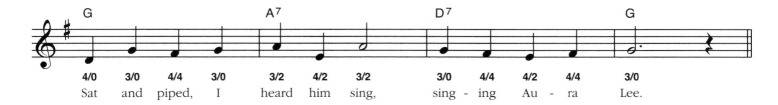

Sat and piped, I heard him sing, sing-ing Au-ra Lee.

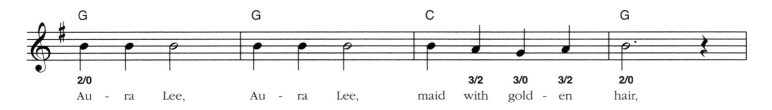

Au-ra Lee, Au-ra Lee, maid with gold-en hair,

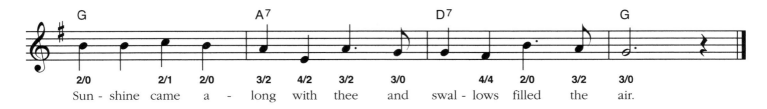

Sun-shine came a-long with thee and swal-lows filled the air.

STRUM NO. 7

The type of arpeggio strum described in Strum No. 6 adapts very well to $\frac{3}{4}$ time. This strum is used for gentle waltzes and other slow to moderate tempos. Count "*one* and *two* and *three* and." Here's how to do it:

1st beat

Thumb picks down on fifth or fourth string.

and

Index picks up on third string.

2nd beat

Middle finger picks up on second string.

and

Ring finger picks up on first string.

3rd beat

Middle finger picks up on second string.

and

Index picks up on third string.

Summing up, each measure of $\frac{3}{4}$ time is played as follows:

1	and	2	and	3	and
Thumb picks down on fifth or fourth string	Index picks up on third string	Middle picks up on second string	Ring picks up on first string	Middle picks up on second string	Index picks up on third string

Once you know this strum and can do it nice and smoothly, try this typical $\frac{3}{4}$ time cowboy song. The melody is the same as "My Bonnie Lies Over the Ocean," but the words are from the American West.

The chords used in this song are:

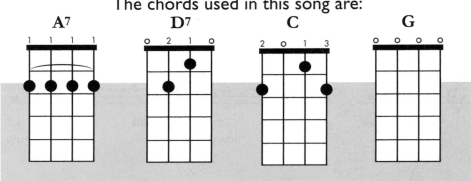

A7   D7   C   G

The Cowboy's Dream

Track 39

American Cowboy Song

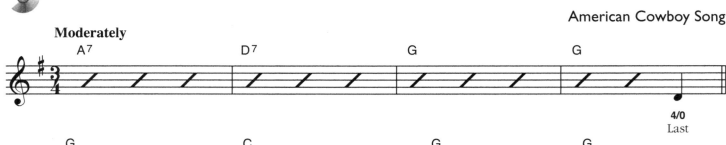

Moderately

A7   D7   G   G

4/0
Last

G   C   G   G

| 2/0 | 3/2 | 3/0 | 3/2 | 3/0 | 4/2 | 4/0 | 2/0 | | 4/0 |
| night | as | I | lay | on | the | prair - ie | | | and |

*This note is played 8va higher.

STRUM NO. 8

This famous banjo strum is used for $\frac{2}{4}$ or cut time tempos such as fiddle tunes, hoedowns and other fast dances. In addition to picking down on a string with the thumb (which you've already been doing),

this Strum No. 8 uses a technique called the **double scratch**. Keep your right hand poised over the head of the banjo. You can rest it lightly on the ring finger if this helps steady your hand (Photo 1).

Now scratch down with the fingernail of the right-hand index finger. No need to strike all the strings; the two or three highest will suffice (Photo 2). Then scratch up with the index finger (Photo 3).

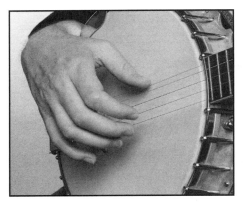

▲ *Right hand poised over banjo head*

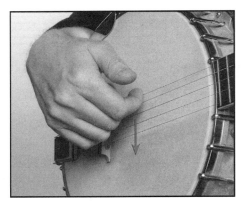

▲ *Index scratches down*

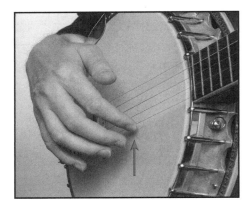

▲ *Index scratches up*

1st beat

Thumb picks down on fifth or fourth string.

uh

Do nothing.

and

Index finger scratches down.

uh

Index finger scratches up.

2nd beat

Thumb picks down on fifth or fourth string. (Choose a different string than the one you played on the first beat.)

uh

Do nothing.

and

Index finger scratches down.

uh

Index finger scratches up.

Summing up, the two beats in a $\frac{2}{4}$ or cut time measure are played like this:

1	and	uh	2	and	uh
Thumb picks down on fifth or fourth string	Index scratches down across top strings	Index scratches up across top strings	Thumb picks down on fifth or fourth	Index scratches down across top strings	Index scratches up across top strings

As usual, practice the strum slowly till it sounds smooth. Then gradually bring it up to a nice, moderately fast tempo. Finally, play it on all the different chords you've learned.

The chords used in this song are:

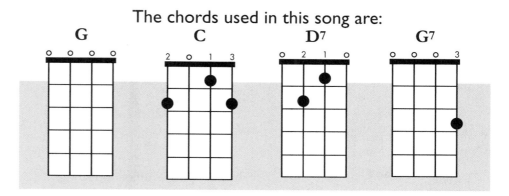

Use Strum No. 8 to accompany this country classic.

New River Train

Track 40

Brightly

American Folk Song

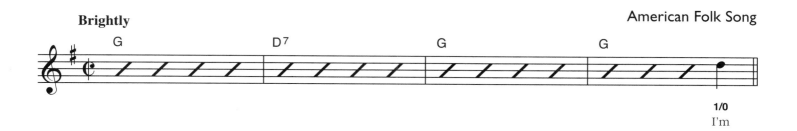

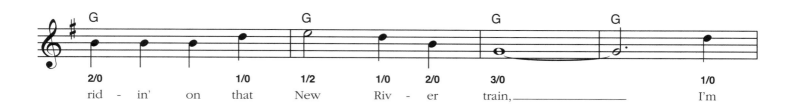

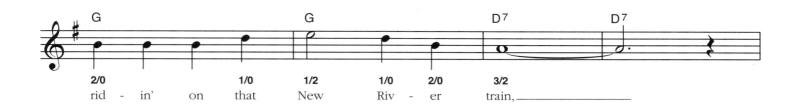

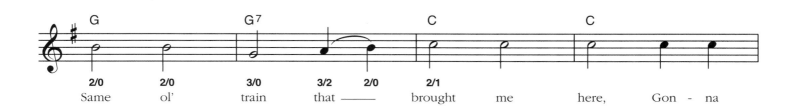

STRUM NO. 9

The double scratch works nicely in $\frac{3}{4}$ time also. Start by counting *"one* and *two* and *three* and." Then put the strum together like this:

1st beat	2nd beat	3rd beat
Thumb picks down on fifth or fourth string.	Index scratches down on top strings.	Index scratches down on top strings.
and	**and**	**and**
Do nothing	Index scratches up on top strings.	Do nothing

Summing up, each measure of $\frac{3}{4}$ time is played:

1	and	2	and	3	and
Thumb picks down on fifth or fourth string	(Hold)	Index scratches down on higher strings	Index scratches up on higher strings	Index scratches down on higher strings	(Hold)

The chords used in this song are:

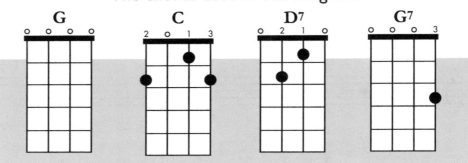

Because of its somewhat rowdy sound, this isn't the best strum for pretty ballads or sad cowboy songs. Instead, restrict its use to rollicking waltzes like this one!

Daisy Bell  **Track 41**
(A Bicycle Built for Two)

Harry Dacre

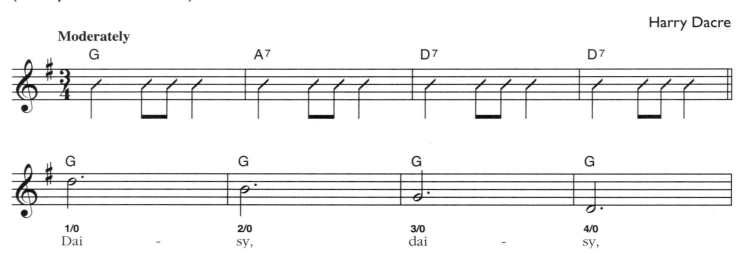

1/0	2/0	3/0	4/0
Dai -	sy,	dai -	sy,

MELODY PLAYING

In many songs you can bring out the melody by picking a certain string in a chord or by playing a series of single notes. Although it's neither necessary nor advisable to play the melody while you're singing, an instrumental chorus (melody on banjo with no singing) can come as a welcome change in the middle of several vocal choruses.

One way to play the melody is to pick it with your thumb. The only difference between this style of melody playing and Strum No. 8 is that instead of playing only the fifth or fourth string, the thumb now plays the melody. Since the melody note is usually found

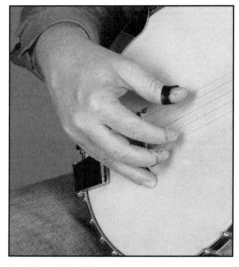

▲ *Thumb pick*

within the chord, this means that you'll already be fingering the note you want. Places that simply hold

the melody note are filled in by a double scratch.

In order to make the melody stand out louder than the scratch strokes, players use a **thumb pick.** This piece of plastic fits over your thumb.

By striking the melody notes with the thumb pick, the melody is automatically accented.

Here are a few examples on the G, D7 and C chords. Notice that the melody notes are labeled with a fraction that tells you where to play them: 2/0 = second string open; 3/2 = third string, second fret; and

so on. The scratch strokes are indicated with linked slash marks:

Remember to hold the chord while you do the scratch strokes.

Playing the next arrangement will put this technique to practical use.

Goodnight Ladies Track 45

The chords used in this song are:

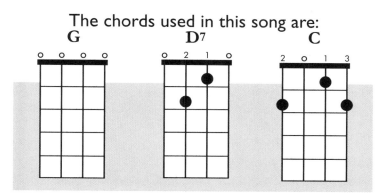

American Folk Song

Moderately

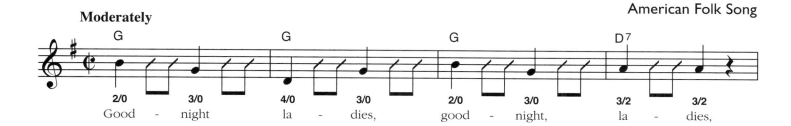

Good - night la - dies, good - night, la - dies,

good - night, la - dies, we're goin' to leave you now.

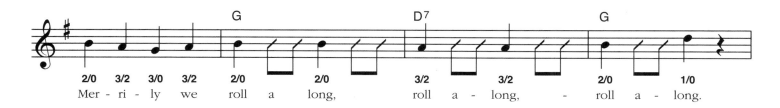

Mer - ri - ly we roll a long, roll a - long, - roll a long.

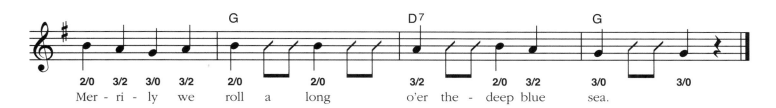

Mer - ri - ly we roll a long o'er the - deep blue sea.

Additional words:

1.

Fare-well, la-dies,

Fare-well, la-dies,

Fare-well, la-dies,

We're goin' to leave you now.

2.

Sweet dreams, la-dies,

Sweet dreams, la-dies,

Sweet dreams, la-dies,

We're goin' to leave you now.

Here's a good old country song that was made for melody playing. Once you've learned the fingering, work the tempo up to $\downarrow$ =120 if possible.

My Home's Across the Smoky Mountains

Track 46

The chords used in this song are:

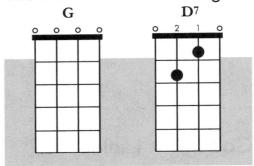

American Folk Song

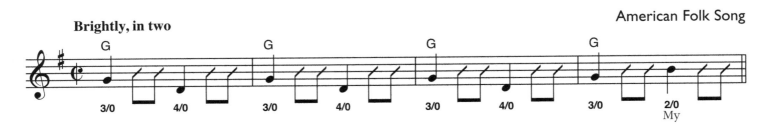

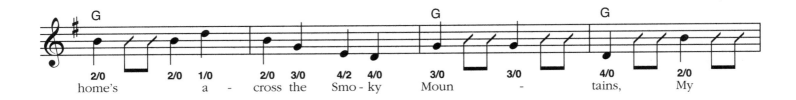

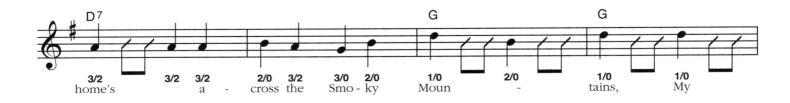

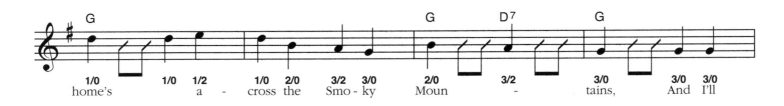

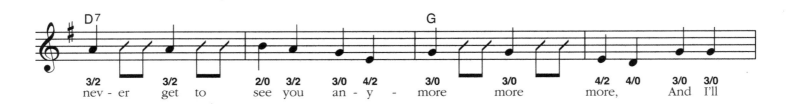

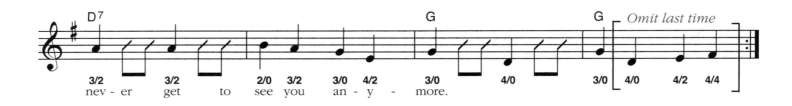

The chords used in this song are:

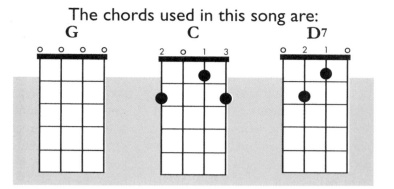

Another old-time country favorite, this time from the Ozarks. This also works well with melody picking.

Lolly Too Dum Track 47

American Folk Song

Moderately bright, in two

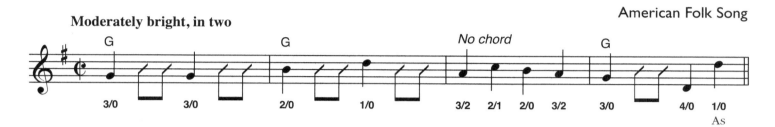

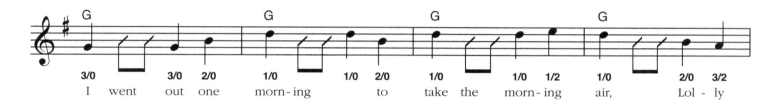

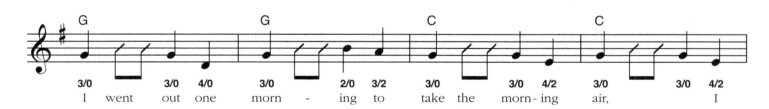

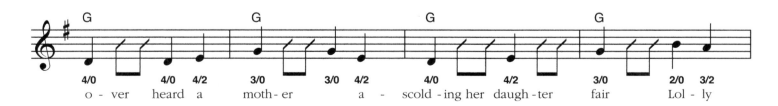

HAMMERING-ON

Hammering-on is a wonderful effect that can be used to enhance both accompaniments and melody picking. The hammer-on is accomplished by snapping a left-hand finger down hard and fast to produce a sound without using the right hand at all.

Try it now: Hammer the third finger of the left hand down on the first string, third fret. You should hear the F note sound clear and almost as loud as if you had picked it with the right hand. If the note doesn't sound clear, make sure you hammer directly behind (not on) the third fret, and that you keep the pressure on the string once the finger is down.

Now use the third finger to hammer the second string, third fret. Next, use the second finger to hammer the third string, second fret. Finally, use the second finger to hammer the fourth string, second fret. (Notice that we don't use the first finger to hammer on. This is because unless you have a top-of-the-line banjo, it's difficult to bring out any hammered note on the first fret.) In this book we'll use the letter "H" to indicate a hammered note as in the following exercise.

Track 48

Hammering-on is particularly effective when preceded by an open string, as in the following exercise. Only hammer the notes marked with an H. All other notes are picked with the right-hand index finger.

Track 49

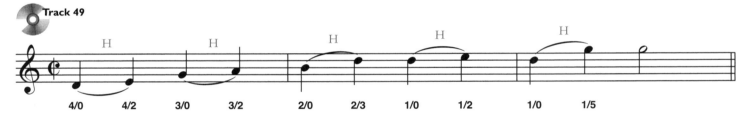

Track 50

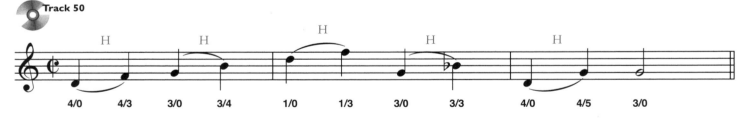

Now, combine open strings, hammered notes, and the double scratch into this variation on Strum No. 8. (You may want to review Strum No. 8—it's on page 40.) Notice that there are two spots in the strum in which the player is instructed to "do nothing." You can now fill these spots with a hammered note. This produces the following strum which we'll call No. 8a.

1	uh	and	uh	2	uh	and	uh
Thumb picks down on fourth or third string	Hammer-on that string	Index scratches down	Index scratches up	Thumb picks down on fourth or third string	Hammer-on that string	Index scratches down	Index scratches up

The chords used in this song are:

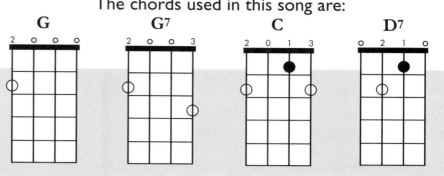

Take a minute to study the chords used in this song. The notes marked with an open circle are those which can be used for hammering-on. Especially notice that the G chord has an added note so you can hammer it.

Come and Go with Me Track 51

African-American Gospel Song

Moderately fast

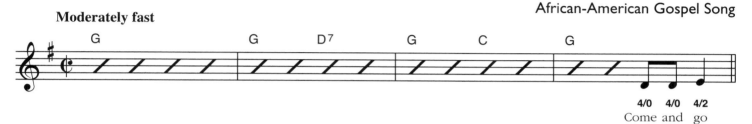

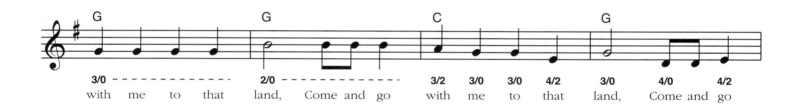

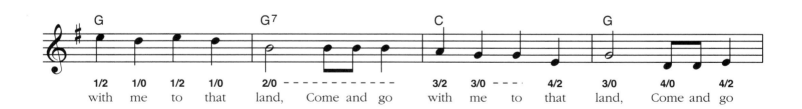

MINI MUSIC LESSON
PULLING-OFF

A complementary technique to hammering-on is called **pulling-off**. It, too, can be used to enhance accompaniment or melody picking. Here's how to do it.

Use the third finger on the left hand to finger the first string, third fret. Pick the first string with the index finger of the right hand. This produces the note F. Now, without using the right hand, pull the third finger away from the fingerboard so that the open first string sounds. You can't just pick up the finger; you must pull it sideways so that the open string sounds clear.

Once you can pull-off on the first string, try it with various other notes, such as the second string, third fret; the third string, second fret; the fourth string, second fret. We'll use the letter "P" to mark the places where a pull-off is desired.

Try this new technique on an old square dance tune. It uses pulling-off and, in a few places, hammering-on. Also notice that the B note is played in an alternative place—the third string, fourth fret. But use the third finger to play it.

Pete Seeger, who has composed over 100 songs, uses a straightforward melodic and harmonic style. Although an accomplished banjo player, Seeger emphasized the functional supportive accompaniment of the banjo rather than its virtuosity. *Photo courtesy of Country Music Foundation.*

Cotton-Eyed Joe Track 52

No chords are used in this arrangement.

American Square Dance Tune

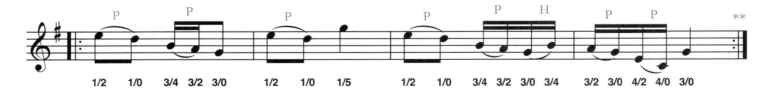

This is an example of pull-offs and hammer-ons used in solo melody playing.

* This repeat sign means to go back and play again from the beginning.

** This second repeat means to go back and play again from the earlier repeat.

STRUM NO. 8b

Pulling-off can be incorporated into strum No. 8 to produce a strum we'll call No. 8b. Here's how to do it:

1	uh	and	uh	2	uh	and	uh
Thumb picks down on fifth, fourth or third string	Pull-off any note	Index scratches down	Index scratches up	Thumb picks down on fifth, fourth or third string	Pull-off any note	Index scratches down	Index scratches up

Use Strum No. 8b to accompany this great old country tune.

The Old Gray Mare Track 53

The chords used in this song are:

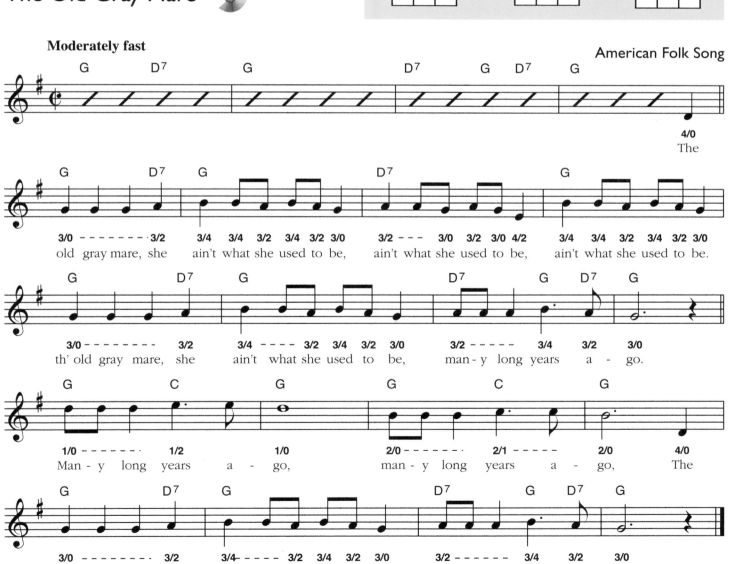

BLUEGRASS

Bluegrass music developed in the 1920s. Some think it came about as an outgrowth of country players using stringed instruments such as banjo, mandolin, fiddle, bass and guitar to imitate what they heard on Dixieland jazz records.

The Bluegrass style was perfected by the great Earl Scruggs in the 1940s. Bluegrass is more popular than ever, and the virtuoso banjo players active today are too numerous to mention. A detailed study of bluegrass style is really beyond the scope of this book, but we'll give you a taste of what it is and how to play it.

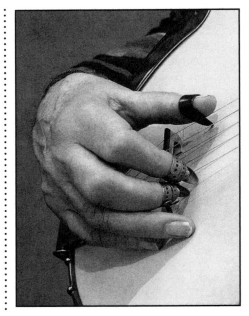

▲ *Finger picks*

Bluegrass is played wearing a thumb pick (see photo on page 44) and two finger picks. Take some time at your local music store and choose picks that fit perfectly. They should neither be so loose so that they slide around on your fingers, nor should they be so tight that you can't slide them on all the way. Notice that the finger picks jut out a little past the tips of the fingers.

The basic bluegrass strum is called a **roll**. It is always in $\frac{4}{4}$ time, counted "*one* and *two* and *three* and *four*" and. Unlike strums you have learned, however, bluegrass rolls divide the eight counts as 3 + 3 + 2. This gives the roll an exciting rhythmic push which musicians call *syncopation*. Try the following at a very slow tempo.

Bluegrass Roll No. I

1	and	2	and	3	and	4	and
Index plays second string	Middle plays first string	Thumb plays fifth string	Index plays second string	Middle plays first string	Thumb plays fifth string	Index plays second string	Middle plays first string

For the proper syncopated effect, accent the notes on the first beat, the *and* of 2, and the fourth beat. In this roll, this means accent every note played by the index finger. Once you get the strum working smoothly on an open G chord (and we recommend using a metronome to keep the beat steady), start picking up the tempo. Bluegrass requires fast reflexes, because the music is often played at a blazing speed. Tempos of over 200 beats per minute are not at all unusual!

Next, play the roll on all the chords you know. Hammering-on and pulling-off can, and should, be used to give variety to the chords being played.

Okay, it's time to play some bluegrass! Make sure you can do the roll on the previous page at a reasonably fast tempo. Then try it on this country favorite.

The first time through use the plain chords (we've picked a tune that uses only two). The second time, try adding some hammer-ons and pull-offs. Then check out the bottom of this page for a variation on the basic roll.

The chords used in this song are:

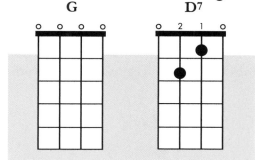

Black-Eyed Susie

American Folk Song

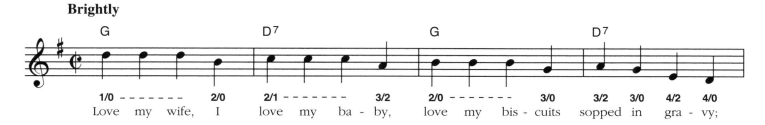

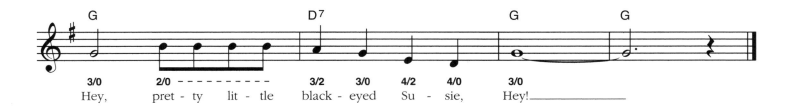

Bluegrass Roll No. 1a

This roll is identical to Roll No. 1, except that the index and middle fingers now play the third and second strings respectively. Once you can play this roll at a fairly quick tempo, try it out on *Black-Eyed Susie*.

1	and	2	and	3	and	4	and
Index plays third string	Middle plays second string	Thumb plays fifth string	Index plays third string	Middle plays second string	Thumb plays fifth string	Index plays third string	Middle plays second string

The chords used in this song are:

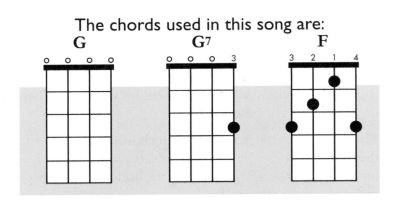

Use either of the basic rolls you have learned to play this all-time bluegrass favorite. Also notice we're introducing a new chord—the F chord.

Old Joe Clark

Track 55

American Folk Song

Brightly

Verse: G · G7 · G · G · G7 · G

1/0 1/2 1/3 1/2 1/0 2/1 2/0 3/0 1/0 1/2 1/3 1/2 1/0 3/0
I went up to old Joe's house, old Joe was not at home. I

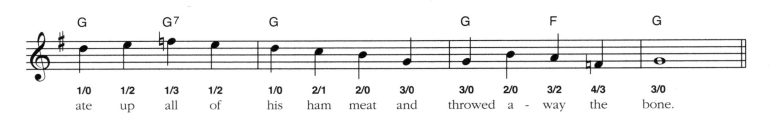

G · G7 · G · G · F · G

1/0 1/2 1/3 1/2 1/0 2/1 2/0 3/0 3/0 2/0 3/2 4/3 3/0
ate up all of his ham meat and throwed a - way the bone.

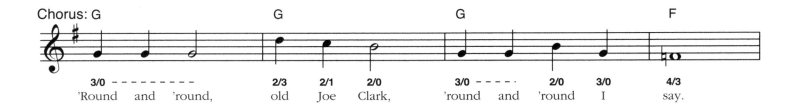

Chorus: G · G · G · F

3/0 - - - - - - - - 2/3 2/1 2/0 3/0 - - - - - 2/0 3/0 4/3
'Round and 'round, old Joe Clark, 'round and 'round I say.

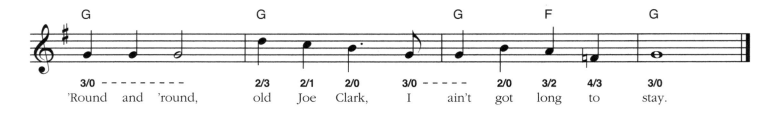

G · G · G · F · G

3/0 - - - - - - - - 2/3 2/1 2/0 3/0 - - - - - 2/0 3/2 4/3 3/0
'Round and 'round, old Joe Clark, I ain't got long to stay.

Additional verses:

1.
Old Joe Clark had a house, 'twas fifteen stories high,

And ev'ry story of that house was filled
   with chicken pie.

(Repeat Chorus)

2.
Old Joe's got an old red cow, got a bell
   around her neck,

If she ever gets in my cornfield, I'll shoot
   her all to heck.

(Repeat Chorus)

Bluegrass (cont'd)

All bluegrass rolls use the same basic rhythm, so variety is achieved by changing the order of the picking fingers. In another common bluegrass roll the thumb leads off, followed by the index and middle fingers.

Bluegrass Roll No. 2

1	and	2	and	3	and	4	and
Thumb plays fifth string	Index plays second string	Middle plays first string	Thumb plays fifth string	Index plays second string	Middle plays first string	Index plays second string	Middle plays first string

The chords used in this song are:

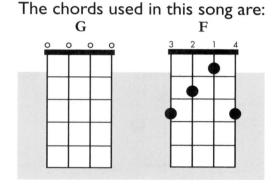

When you've got Roll No. 2 worked up to tempo try it on this bluegrass standard.

Little Maggie Track 56

Important note: You can use any roll on any bluegrass tune. You can also mix the different rolls on the same tune, and even the same measure if your reflexes are good that day. And don't forget to vary the chords with hammer-ons and pull-offs!

 C TUNING

Although the G tuning is the easiest and most common tuning of the five-string banjo, there are many other possible tunings that can be used for certain keys and special effects. All the songs you've played so far have been in the G tuning. The **C tuning** is the same as the G tuning except that the fourth string is tuned down a full tone from D to the note C.

Tuning to a Keyboard

Counting middle C as one, find the C below middle C, which is the eighth white key to the left. Tune the fourth string to this note.

Tuning to a Pitch Pipe or **Electronic Tuner**

Tune the fourth string to the C below middle C.

Tuning Relatively

Tune the fourth string at the seventh fret to the third string open. Or, tune the open fourth string an octave below the second string, first fret. (Remember that an octave is the sound of the first two notes of the song "Over the Rainbow.")

Whatever method you use for tuning, you'll wind up with the banjo tuned: **G C G B D**

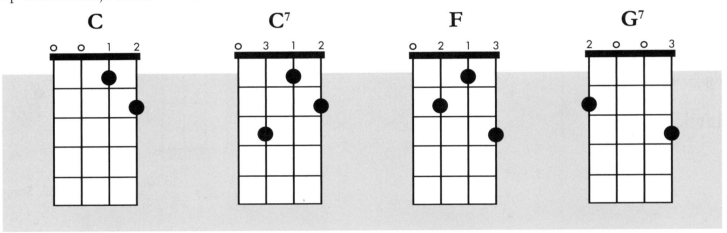

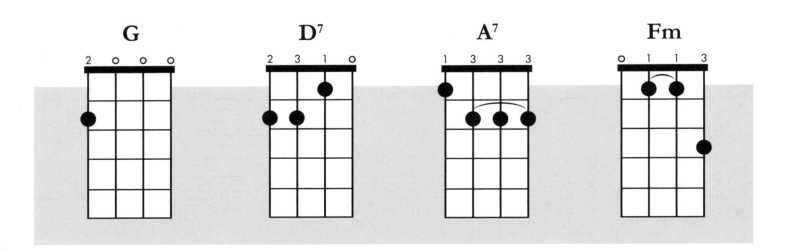

Since the note on the fourth string has changed, this means that the chords in the C tuning will be slightly different from the same chords in G tuning. Here are a few basic chords in the C tuning.

The chords used in this song are:

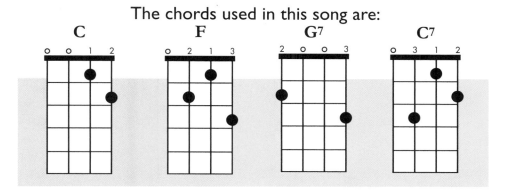

In general, the C tuning is used for songs in the key of C, like this great old railroad song. Use Strums 8, 8a, and/or 8b to accompany it.

The Wabash Cannonball

 Track 57

American Folk Song

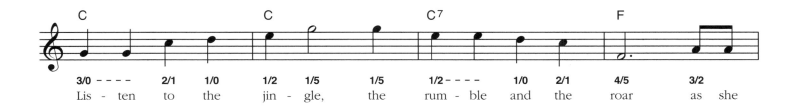

3/0 - - - -   2/1   1/0   1/2   1/5   1/5   1/2 - - - -   1/0   2/1   4/5   3/2
Lis - ten   to   the   jin - gle,   the   rum - ble   and   the   roar   as she

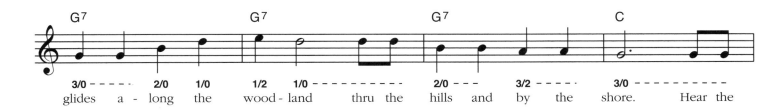

3/0 - - - - -   2/0   1/0   1/2   1/0 - - - - - - - - -   2/0 - - -   3/2 - - - - -   3/0 - - - - - - - - -
glides   a - long   the   wood - land   thru the   hills   and   by   the   shore.   Hear the

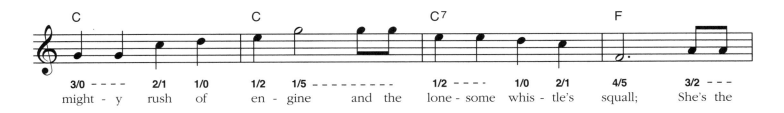

3/0 - - - -   2/1   1/0   1/2   1/5 - - - - - - -   1/2 - - - -   1/0   2/1   4/5   3/2 - - -
might - y   rush   of   en - gine   and the   lone - some   whis - tle's   squall;   She's the

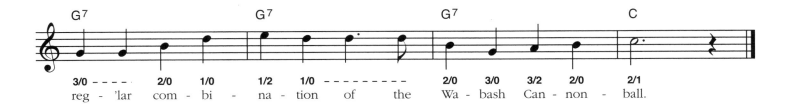

3/0 - - - -   2/0   1/0   1/2   1/0 - - - - - - - - -   2/0   3/0   3/2   2/0   2/1
reg - 'lar   com - bi - na - tion   of   the   Wa - bash   Can - non - ball.**

The chords used in this song are:

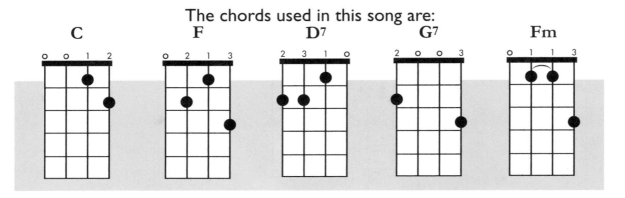

For this next folk classic we suggest using Strum No. 7 (see page 38). Study the chords carefully before playing the song. **Note:** The abbreviation "Fm" stands for the F minor chord.

Home on the Range **Track 58**

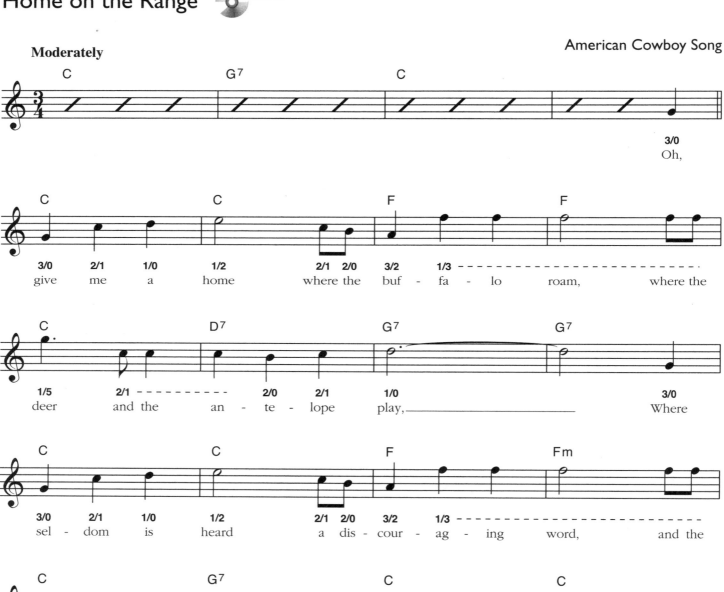

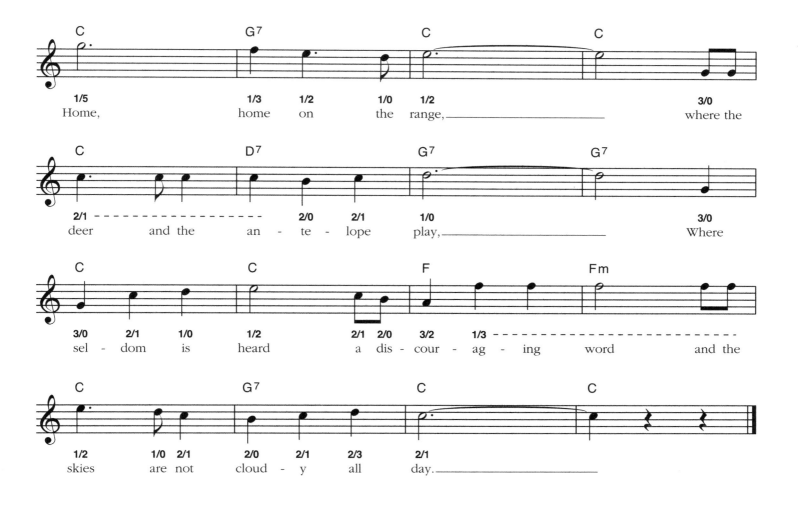

STRUM NO. 10

This strum introduces a technique called the **pinch**. In the pinch, the thumb picks down and a different finger, usually the middle finger, picks up simultaneously. Here's how to do it in $\frac{3}{4}$ time. Notice the pinch on the first beat.

1	and	2	and	3	and
Thumb picks down on fifth string **and** middle picks up on first string	Index picks up on third string	Middle picks up on second string	Index picks up on third string	Middle picks up on first string	Index picks up on third string

Notice that the index finger always plays the third string, but the middle finger moves back and forth between the first and second strings. It's a little tricky, but well worth the effort.

Once you can do the strum smoothly and evenly use it to accompany "Home on the Range" and other songs in $\frac{3}{4}$ time.

Track 59

TRANSPOSITION

O.K., so now you can play songs in the keys of G and C. So you go into your local music store and buy a collection of your favorite tunes and (gasp!) you discover that many of them are in neither of the keys you know. Don't panic. The answer to this problem lies in *transposition*. Transposition means to take a song written in one key and play it in a different key. The chart below will show you how to do it. Your object is to transpose every song into the key of G or the key of C, whichever fits your voice better.

First, you must determine the key of the song you're looking at. This is easy to do. Simply look at the last chord in the song. If the last chord is a C chord, the song is most likely in the key of C. If it's an E♭ chord, the song is probably in the key of E♭, and so on.

Next, find the key in the first column. Let's take E♭ as an example. In the first column E♭ is found in row four. To transpose from E♭ to C, every note in row four is moved directly upward to row one. Thus, the E♭ chord is played as a C chord, the A♭ chord is played as

an F chord and the B♭7 chord is played as a G7 chord.

If you want to transpose from E♭ to G, all the notes in row four are moved directly down to row eight. Now the E♭ chord becomes G, the A♭ chord becomes C, and the B♭7 chord becomes D7.

Using the same method, *any* song in *any* key can be transposed to the key of G or the key of C.

1.	C	C♯/D♭	D	E♭	E	F	F♯/G♭	G	A♭	A	B♭	B
2.	C♯/D♭	D	E♭	E	F	F♯/G♭	G	A♭	A	B♭	B	C
3.	D	E♭	E	F	F♯/G♭	G	A♭	A	B♭	B	C	C♯/D♭
4.	E♭	E	F	F♯/G♭	G	A♭	A	B♭	B	C	C♯/D♭	D
5.	E	F	F♯/G♭	G	A♭	A	B♭	B	C	C♯/D♭	D	E♭
6.	F	F♯/G♭	G	A♭	A	B♭	B	C	C♯/D♭	D	E♭	E
7.	F♯/G♭	G	A♭	A	B♭	B	C	C♯D♭	D	E♭	E	F
8.	G	A♭	A	B♭	B	C	C♯/D♭	D	E♭	E	F	F♯/G♭
9.	A♭	A	B♭	B	C	C♯/D♭	D	E♭	E	F	F♯/G♭	G
10.	A	B♭	B	C	C♯/D♭	D	E♭	E	F	F♯/G♭	G	A♭
11.	B♭	B	C	C♯/D♭	D	E♭	E	F	F♯/G♭	G	A♭	A
12.	B	C	C♯/D♭	D	E♭	E	F	F♯/G♭	G	A♭	A	B♭

THE CAPO

All the songs in this book have been in either the key of G or the key of C.

The **capo** (pronounced KAY-po) is a device that allows you to play in other keys without learning any new chord positions. Here's how it works:

Clamp the capo across the first, second, third or fourth fret. Notice that to get the best sound, the capo must be slightly behind the fret, not directly on it. See the first photo below. Let's say you have chosen to place the capo on the second fret. This means that the banjo is now tuned in the key of A. (We'll get to what to do about the fifth string in a moment.) Play your open G chord. It now sounds like an A chord. The D7 has become an E7, the C chord has become a D chord and so on. All you have to do is imagine that the capo is a temporary nut, and play the chords you already know. See for example how the D7 chord fingering looks with the capo on the second fret.

▲ *The capo*

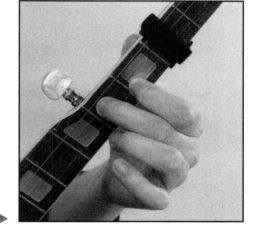

Playing the D7 chord fingering with the capo on the second fret (The chord sounds as an E7) ▶

What to Do About the 5th String

In the G tuning the fifth string is tuned to G, the root or name of the key. In the C tuning the fifth string is tuned to the fifth note of the key, G. (C =1 , D = 2, E = 3, F = 4, G = 5) In order to keep these relationships intact, the fifth string must be retuned. If the capo is placed on the first fret, tune the fifth string a half step higher to A♭. This is the fourth black key above middle C on your keyboard. If the capo is placed on the second fret, tune the fifth string a whole step higher to A, which is the white key directly to the right of the A♭ key.

If you want to place the capo any higher, you'll need to have your local technician install a small screw in the fingerboard which allows you to slip the fifth string under it. Otherwise, tuning the fifth string any higher will cause it to break. Some banjos have a small fifth string capo which can be adjusted for virtually any key.

The following chart shows the keys available by using the capo.

In the G tuning
No capo = key of G
Capo on 1st fret = key of A♭
Capo on 2nd fret = key of A
Capo on 3rd fret = key of B♭
Capo on 4th fret = key of B

In the C tuning
No capo = key of C
Capo on 1st fret = key of D♭
Capo on 2nd fret = key of D
Capo on 3rd fret = key of E♭
Capo on 4th fret = key of E

CHORDS IN G TUNING

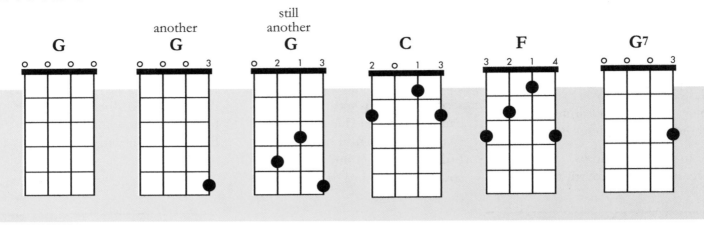

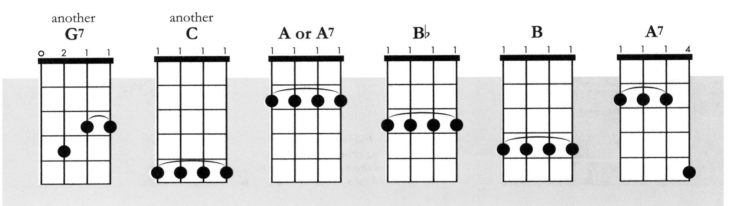

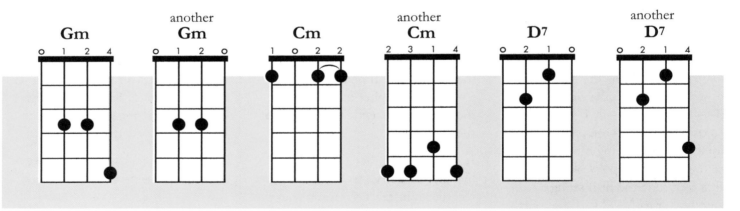

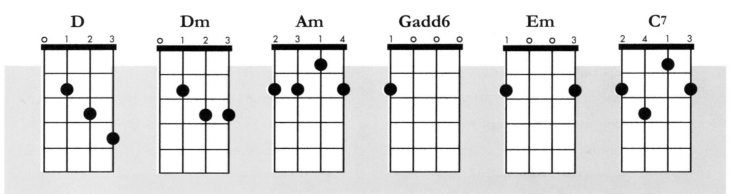

CHORDS IN C TUNING

Note: On chords marked with an asterisk, avoid playing the short fifth string.

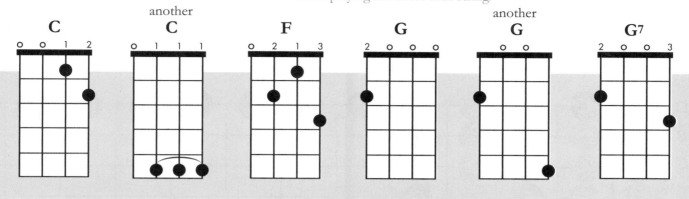

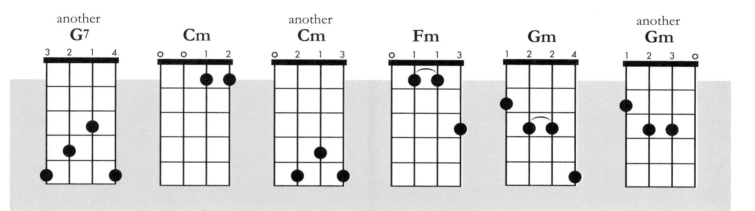

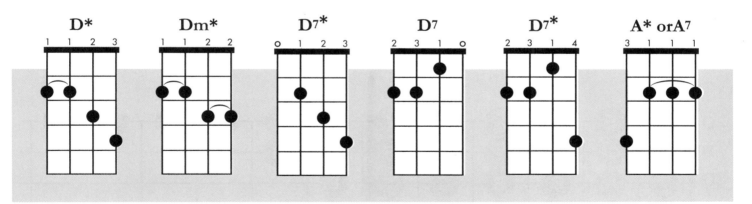

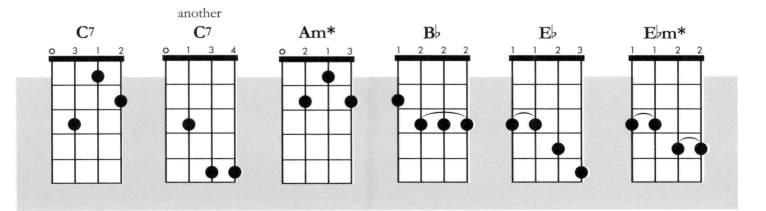

FINGERING CHART IN G TUNING

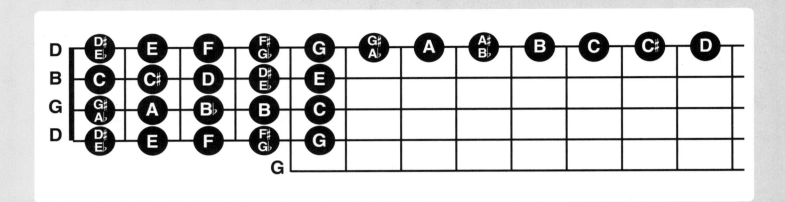

FINGERING CHART IN C TUNING

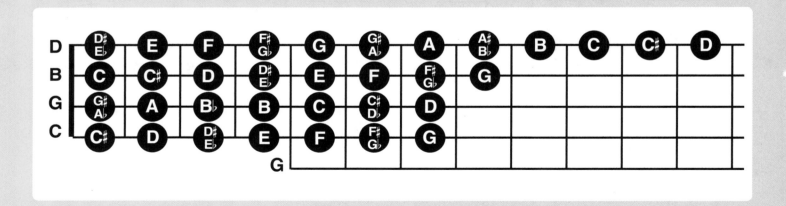